Night-vision
goggles

Hand-held
transmitter

Laptop computer
trace showing
presence of bug
in a building

James Bond's
piton gun from
*Goldeneye*

Side view of
explosives pack for
stay-behind agents
in the event of World
War III occurring

Ultraviolet
lantern and
anti-bugging
seals

Prints made by SOE agent's rubber
soles used to disguise beach landings

Ox tongue tin for
smuggling maps and
compasses, World War I

# EYEWITNESS GUIDES

# SPY

German invisible ink
and sponge

Written by
**Richard Platt**

Photographed by

**Geoff Dann and Steve Gorton**

SOE rubber soles
worn on boots to
disguise landings on
beaches and in deserts

Leather boot heel
with concealed
compartment,
World
War II

Message hidden
in rubber boot
heel, World
War II

## DK

**DORLING KINDERSLEY**
London • New York • Stuttgart

Counter-espionage mirror for looking round corners

Transmitter for bugging room

Silk map of France used by wartime agent

**DK**

## A DORLING KINDERSLEY BOOK

**Project editor** Miranda Smith
**Art editor** Kati Poynor
**Assistant editor** Julie Ferris
**Managing editor** Gillian Denton
**Managing art editor** Julia Harris
**Production** Charlotte Traill
**Picture research** Sarah Moule

This Eyewitness ® Guide has been conceived by
Dorling Kindersley Limited and Editions Gallimard

First published in Great Britain in 1996
by Dorling Kindersley Limited,
9 Henrietta Street, London WC2E 8PS
Reprinted 1997

A CIP catalogue record for this book is
available from the British Library.

ISBN 0 7513 6076 7

Colour reproduction by
Colourscan, Singapore
Printed in Singapore by Toppan

Hand-held transmitter or "bug"

Doll made in Fresnes prison by World War II agent Odette Sampson

Matchbox created for Special Operations Executive agent

# Contents

Capsule for
suicide pill,
World War II

Suicide pill,
World War II

Hand-held
receiver and
earpiece

# What is a spy?

SPYING, WHICH IS ALSO called espionage, began thousands of years ago, with nations battling for land, wealth or slaves. Spies sneaked into the camps of their enemies, counting the number of warriors, or looking for plans of attack. If they were successful, they returned as heroes with the intelligence – the secrets – they had uncovered. Those who failed and were caught, faced execution. Throughout history, generals, governments, and business people have used words like "TOP SECRET" and "CONFIDENTIAL" to guard important data or documents. Spies are employed by such people to find out information that enemies would rather keep hidden, and pass secrets to people who were not originally intended to know them. Today spies still live dangerous lives. Some work like burglars to collect intelligence. Others have access to secrets only because other people trust them. By betraying that trust, a spy can win or lose wars, and even change the course of history.

*Rahab marked her windows with a red cord*

*Joshua watches as the walls of Jericho tumble down*

*Tapestry shows spies from both sides in the Battle of Hastings*

**BIBLE ESPIONAGE**
A story in the Old Testament, the holy book of Judaism and Christianity, tells how spies helped defeat the walled city of Jericho. The leader of the attacking army, Joshua, sent two spies into the town at dusk. They went to the house of a prostitute, Rahab, and hid on the roof. Rahab lied to the Jericho authorities to protect the spies, and when Joshua's troops destroyed the city, they spared the lives of Rahab and her family, but killed everybody else.

**EGYPTIAN SPY**
Ankhesenamen, young queen of Egypt, wanted to remarry when her husband Tutankhamen died in 1340 BC. She wrote to a neighbouring king: "Send me one of your grown-up sons ... he shall be king over Egypt." Instead, the king sent his assistant as a spy to check the queen's story.

## SPYING FOR THE MONGOLS

Spies helped Genghis Khan (1162–1227) to conquer most of Asia. Khan came from Mongolia in central Asia, but he knew that people from Mongolia would soon arouse suspicion in distant lands. So he shrewdly recruited spies from among the target peoples, and these local spies were able to move around freely collecting intelligence. Over longer distances, he used horsemen who could ride ten times faster than an army could march to carry his secret messages.

*In the east, the Mongol empire reached the Pacific*

## ALEXANDER THE GREAT

The Macedonian king Alexander the Great (356–323 BC) used spies to find out about enemies' troop movements, and also to scout the best marching routes for his massive armies. Alexander's spies used a simple but effective technique to keep their messages secret. They wrote on narrow scrolls spiralling around a stick. Unwinding the scroll broke up the words of the message. But, wound around an identical stick, the text was easy to read.

*The Bayeux Tapestry is actually embroidery on a linen strip 70 m (230 ft) long*

## UNNOTICED IN THE CROWD

Some of the greatest spies of the past have been female: women could often go unnoticed where a man would arouse suspicion. In wartime, almost all young men joined the armed forces, and a man in civilian clothes was an unusual sight. In this photograph of Dutch spies at work during World War II (1939–45), one of the women takes a picture with a hidden camera.

*Patterned bag hides camera lens*

*No peacetime spy has 007's "licence to kill"*

## RECORDED FOR POSTERITY

The Bayeux Tapestry shows spies in the historic Battle of Hastings in England in 1066. The tapestry records how an army from northwest France, led by William of Normandy (1028–1087), conquered England in 1066. English spies reported sighting thousands of clean-shaven men with short hair. At that time in England, all men except priests wore moustaches and long hair, so the spies assumed that they had seen thousands of French priests. In fact, these "priests" were soldiers who greatly outnumbered the English.

## FICTIONAL SPIES

Glamorous spy James Bond, agent 007, is the hero of 13 novels by English author Ian Lancaster Fleming (1908–64). Fleming was himself a spy before he began his career as a writer. He used the people he met during that time as models for the characters in his books. The plots of the books and the Bond films leave out the routine side of the lives of real spies. However, some of Fleming's own exploits were as daring as those of the fictional agent 007.

# Types of spy

SPIES COME FROM many different backgrounds and are recruited by an espionage agency for a variety of reasons. Many spies are attracted by money but some are led by deeply-held beliefs and are called "walk-in" spies because they require no persuasion. Others spy because they are being blackmailed, and still more because it makes them feel important. "Plants" penetrate (work their way into) a target organization where they can collect intelligence. However, recruiting an "agent in place" is sometimes easier than penetration. These trusted insiders have access to secrets even before an agency recruits them – perhaps by using bribery or blackmail.

**TROUBADOURS**
These medieval minstrels went from castle to castle entertaining European nobles. Some spied by listening to royal gossip and repeating the news when they travelled to another country.

*Walker tramped Vienna's streets while Soviet agents checked that he was not being followed*

*Building (indicated by red arrow on map) mentioned in Walker's typed instructions for a 1978 visit to Vienna*

KOMET
KÜCHEN

**CARELESS TALK**
Spies do not make themselves obvious by wearing uniforms! This wartime poster warned British citizens that they should not gossip about sons and husbands in the armed forces because "Careless talk costs lives". Bus passengers listening to the conversation might be spies, and could report details of troop movements to the enemy.

**INSIDER TRAPPED**
French ambassador to Moscow Maurice Dejean unknowingly hired spies to work as his driver and maid. They used blackmail to try and turn him into an "agent in place". The plot failed, but Dejean's career was ruined.

**WALK-IN WALKER**
American John Walker worked for the US Navy and sold intelligence to the Soviet Union for 17 years. To meet them for payment and training, his Soviet handlers usually instructed Walker to travel to Vienna, Austria.

*The splendidly-dressed Russian diplomats are "boyars" – members of noble Russian families*

## AMATEUR SPIES
Since Biblical times, traders have kept their eyes and ears open wide when they travelled abroad. These "amateur spies" are returning home from the land of Canaan to report what they had seen.

*Iraq designed the "Supergun" to shell targets thousands of kilometres away*

## EXPENDABLE SPIES
MI6 (the British secret intelligence service) encouraged businesses to sell parts for weapons such as this "Supergun" to Iraq in the 1980s. The exporters brought back intelligence which was highly valued by MI6. However, the exporters were actually breaking an arms ban. The British government tried, and failed, to avoid embarrassment by denying the authorization of the sales.

## MOLE IN THE CIA
Enemy agents who penetrate the security services sometimes earn the nickname of "mole", because they dig deep and work invisibly. Chinese American mole Larry Wu Tai Chin worked for the CIA for more than 35 years. But as a mole he spied for China from the very beginning.

## SPIES AT COURT
Most spies are "illegals" – if they are caught they face prosecution and punishment. Throughout history, traders and merchants, such as the ones in this 16th-century woodcut, have been in a good position to act as "illegals". Diplomats, on the other hand, are often called "legals". These civil servants represent their country in its embassies abroad, and they have a licence to spy. If they are caught, their diplomatic status protects them from punishment under international law. In fact, only very few work as spies. More are intelligence officers – they use their diplomatic jobs as a cover for recruiting and controlling spies.

*Procession of diplomats and merchants at the court of the Austrian archduke Maximilian II*

# Secret tool-kit

A spoof spy kit for the wartime spy

THE CENTRAL INTELLIGENCE AGENCY (CIA) nickname "sneakies" neatly describes the tools, gadgets, and weapons on which undercover agents often rely. With the aid of a sneaky, a spy can bug a conversation or photograph a meeting. Other devices make escape easier, or hide the evidence of espionage from prying eyes. Fictional spy James Bond made sneakies famous. Before a dangerous mission, he visited the workshop of "Q" who built such gadgets. Author Ian Fleming based Q's character on the inventor Charles Fraser Smith (1904–92), who designed the equipment for the British intelligence services in World War II. Other organizations had equally ingenious spy workshops – for example, Stanley Lovell (1890–1976) equipped spies in the United States.

*Pushing the two halves of the camera together advances the film by one frame, and covers the lens*

MINOX EC

*Lens is focused here*

**SUPER SMALL SNAPPER**
The Minox camera is small enough to hide in a fist, but takes photographs of excellent quality. The Latvian manufacturers originally sold the Minox as a pocket-size camera, but the intelligence services quickly realized its potential and it became standard equipment. The camera's only real problem was the tiny size of its negatives which needed to be enlarged 25 times to be read. At this small scale a speck of dust on the film could obscure a vital word.

*Pen writes normally*

**HANDY HEEL**
Concealed items must be well hidden to escape discovery, and shoes and boots can hide quite large weapons or tools. In World War II, spies sometimes concealed gold, for bribery, and knives in their insoles.

*Strip is pulled to withdraw concealed item*

Camera took four pictures when agent uncovered the pinholes

*Exposures lasted minutes, so fixed objects such as buildings were the only practical subjects*

## PINHOLE CAMERA
Some of the tiniest spy cameras use pinholes instead of a lens. KGB agents used this one in the 1980s. The camera takes pictures that are not blurred, however close or far away the object. However, nothing is really sharp either!

*Acoustic tube to microphone*

## LISTENING PEN
The circuits of radio transmitters are now so small that spies can install bugs in the tiniest of objects. This pen is inconspicuous in the pocket, and would not attract attention in a desk drawer. However, it conceals a microphone to eavesdrop on any nearby conversation. A tiny transmitter broadcasts the signal on UHF radio frequencies. The power of the signal is low, but strong enough for an accomplice who may be sitting in a car 500 m (1,640 ft) away to pick up the conversation with a receiver and record it.

*Body of pen conceals transmitter*

## A BRUSH WITH THE ENEMY
All spies risk capture, but the danger is perhaps even greater in wartime. So World War II spies hid all kind of escape equipment in objects like this hairbrush. A compartment contains a saw to cut through prison bars, a map of enemy occupied territory, and a compass.

*Pulling bristles lifts compartment "lid"*

*Tube houses battery with enough power for up to six hours*

*Miniature saw blade*

*Compass*
*Compass needle*

Devices hidden in hairbrush

## EASY ACCESS
The safest way to enter a locked building is to bribe a low-paid employee to unlock the door. Where this is not possible, spies may try to pick the lock with specially shaped tools like these. In Britain, intelligence services employed a retired burglar to teach this vital skill to wartime agents.

*By inserting one of the hooked blades into a lock and turning gently, the tool lifts levers that hold the bolt in place*

*Map printed on thin paper to fold up small*

*Base of brush is hollow*

*Specially-shaped instruments are called picklocks*

*Range of picklocks enables agent to tackle locks of different sizes*

*Picks fold away into penknife-like handle*

## CHEATING AT CARDS
World War II spies concealed an escape map in a pack of playing cards. Tearing each card apart revealed a small area of the map. The numbers on each section allowed the spy to piece the whole map together like a jigsaw.

# Seeing the invisible

VISUAL SURVEILLANCE is part of the training of all agents. They learn to use their eyes and cameras to collect intelligence, or for gathering information to blackmail their enemies. They use technology to make their vision keener. Magnifying lenses give a closer view of private scenes, while some night vision equipment makes photography possible even in a candle-lit bedroom. However, the clearest pictures do not guarantee the success of a surveillance mission. When spies secretly photographed a western diplomat with his girlfriend, they were sure they could use the pictures for blackmail. They met the diplomat and threatened to send the pictures to his wife. His shameless response shocked them. "What wonderful shots!" he exclaimed. "Can you make me copies?"

**NOSY NEIGHBOURS**
The well-equipped spy does not need to stretch to get a better view.

Agent using a night-writing pen

**CAUGHT IN THE ACT**
To photograph subjects in near darkness, spies can use image intensifier cameras. These use a tube similar to those fitted to night-vision equipment (opposite). The camera makes photography possible in extremely dim conditions; the glow of a cigarette provides ample light to photograph an agent copying documents or passing secrets to an accomplice. Image intensifiers cannot record colour, so spies usually load their cameras with sensitive black and white film. In colour (left) pictures have an eerie green glow.

*A spy can swap a standard lens for a powerful telephoto*

*Replacing camera with an eyepiece turns the tube into a night vision telescope*

*Ordinary torch batteries in base provide power*

*Lens enlarges details six times more than a standard lens*

*Lugs for carrying strap*

*"Trigger" operates shutter*

*The rifle grip helps steady camera and keeps photographs sharp where it is impractical to use a tripod*

An ordinary lens takes in the whole of the street market.

Photo-sniper camera picks out two particular figures from the crowd.

*Two small batteries power goggles all night*

*Tubes make light 50,000 times brighter*

*Eyepieces adjust to suit the eyesight of individual spies*

*Head harness is adjustable for comfort*

OH 1×20

*Twin lenses allow spy to judge distance*

*Lenses form life-size images so scene is not distorted and goggles can be used for night-driving*

### SEEING IN THE DARK
Night vision goggles give spies the ability to see in very dim light. In total darkness an infrared torch casts a bright beam upon the scene for anyone wearing the goggles, but nothing can be seen by the target. Details differ, but most systems work like the image-forming tubes used on television cameras. The tube converts photons (packets of light) from the camera lens into electrons (tiny, electrically-charged particles). The electrons speed towards a phosphor screen, making a brilliant glow where they strike it. The screen forms a brighter copy of the original scene.

*Strong harness supports heavy goggles*

Side view of night goggles

*Rifle stock rests against shoulder*

### HAWK EYE
Much surveillance work relies on ordinary cameras and lenses that any wealthy photographer could buy over the counter. However, this powerful 300 mm telephoto lens was specially crafted for use by Soviet border guards and intelligence agents. With it, Soviet spies could close in on a distant scene and photograph agents at work.

### ALL DONE WITH MIRRORS
Spies in 19th-century France used these innocent-looking binoculars to keep a watch on their opponents. One lens produced the same view as an ordinary pair of binoculars. The other was a dummy. Behind it, an angled mirror gave a perfect view of whatever was happening to one side – while the spy appeared to be staring straight ahead. A similar device is still available today. Disguised as a lens hood, it enables spies to photograph subjects at their side, while pointing the camera forwards.

*Real lens*

*Focusing wheel*

*Dummy lens*

*Real lens in side*

*Hole for angled mirror*

# Bugs and taps

BEFORE YOU WHISPER "Tell me!" in a friend's ear, take a careful look around. Whispered words seem secret, but with bugs and wiretaps, spies can make sure that no conversation is really private. Bugs are hidden microphones, usually linked to radio transmitters, and like the insects they are named after, some are tiny. A spy who tunes a radio receiver to the correct frequency can hear every sound that reaches the bug, even if he or she is elsewhere. Telephone bugs or transmitters perform the same service each time a telephone is used. Tape recorders make it easy to monitor (check) wiretaps and bugs. When there is a sound, recording starts automatically, and the tape stops after there have been a few moments of quiet.

**SENDING...**
A basic bug or transmitter can be very small indeed. This one is the size of a matchbox.

**...AND RECEIVING**
This pocket-sized receiver picks up signals from the bug (left), relaying them to headphones or a tape recorder. The bug is a "quick plant" type, small enough to hide behind a picture. Its battery lasts a week. The bug is cheap enough to abandon – returning to collect it doubles the risk of discovery.

The 20-cm (8-in) bug found inside seal

**EMBASSY SEAL**
A gift from the Soviet Union, this replica eagle seal of the United States decorated that country's embassy in Moscow. In fact, the seal housed an ingenious bug. Sound made a spring inside the seal vibrate. Spies in a nearby building were able to detect the vibrations by using radar, and interpret the words that caused the vibrations.

CIA microphone wristwatch

**WHAT IS THE TIME?**
This CIA wristwatch conceals a microphone. It is normally inconspicuous, but in 1977, an American spy in Moscow betrayed himself because he had forgotten to remove his normal watch.

*Link to tape recorder hidden in agent's clothing*

**PHONE-TAPPING**
Telephone taps can be easier to place than bugs because spies need not enter the room they want to listen to. Unless there is a switchboard, a telephone tap can go anywhere between the telephone and the exchange. In this film reconstruction from *Stakeout*, Chris Lecce (played by Richard Dreyfuss) uses a wiretap to keep a vital witness in an organized crime case under surveillance.

**TELEPHONE BUG**
In an office block where there are many extensions and a switchboard, a spy would need to install taps on every outside line and sift through many hours of tapes to hear just one short call. However, if a spy can enter the building unnoticed, a practical solution is possible – fitting a bug to a particular telephone like the one on this page. The spy can then either eavesdrop directly or record conversations and listen at leisure.

*Spy sets transmission frequency here*

**TELEPHONE TRANSMITTER**
A telephone transmitter has the advantage that the "target" picks up the microphone and speaks directly and clearly into it! But the spy hears only the telephone calls, not any other speech in the room.

*Wiretap is connected directly to line*

**WIRETAP**
Sometimes a phone line can be tapped by connecting a couple of wires to leads in the junction box where the telephone line enters the building.

*Telephone tap connected by clips to a chosen line*

*Fibre-optic light-sensing device*

*Flexible antenna broadcasts call to listening spy or recorder*

*Crocodile clip connects to telephone line*

*Transmitter*

*Transmitter*

*Light-sensing device causes transmission to shut down when receiver is replaced*

*Bug powered by lithium is harder to detect than bug that draws power from telephone line*

*Light-sensing switch*

*Microprocessor unit picks up signals from light-sensing device and activates transmitter*

Bugged telephone in transparent casing

MYBELLE SPOTLIGHT

RECALL REDIAL

17

# Listening in

Bugs do not have a great range. In a city a spy must position a receiver within 100–800 m (330–2,625 ft) of the bug to be sure of good reception. Longer ranges are possible in rural areas, where buildings do not obstruct the signal, and where there is less interference from other radio users. The "listening post" – the receiving station – could be in an adjacent building, in a parked car, or even in the spy's pocket. The bug can be hidden in clothing if an agent has arranged a meeting with a contact in a street or park. Supporting agents listen in with cordless earphones.

*Pin-sized antenna*

*Shirt hides induction loop*

*Receiver can switch between two different bugs*

*Tape runs continually throughout the conversation*

## BUG IN THE EAR
With a "neck-tie" of wire, an agent can monitor a bug without wearing conspicuous headphones. The listening device fits in the ear and looks like a hearing aid. The wire round the agent's neck creates an induction loop – a magnetic field that relays the amplified signal from a pocket receiver to the ear.

## WEARING A WIRE
The radio signal from a bug hidden in a spy's clothing can alert counter-espionage agents operating bug detection equipment (pp. 48–49). A miniature tape-recorder gets around the problem because it does not broadcast a radio signal.

*Wearer uses remote switch on microphone to turn tape off*

## A BETTER RECEPTION
Though some general-purpose receivers can pick up bug signals, specially-designed units are often more convenient and provide a better reception. This battery powered model links up with a portable tape recorder for unattended monitoring. An agent who set it up to receive signals from a telephone tap would need to return to the device only occasionally to change the tapes.

*Telescopic antenna*

*Socket for headphones*

*Car battery can power receiver for extended operation*

MON · D  E · TAPE · MANUAL · TAPE · BATT
CHANNEL · RUN · AUTO · POLARITY · LOW
Lorraine Electronics
LONDON
OFF VOLUME
**UXR3**

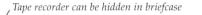
Tape recorder can be hidden in briefcase

*Tiny tape recorder looks like a personal stereo, but has been modified to provide far better sound quality*

*Bug is only 4 mm (0.16 in) thick, and can hide behind a credit card, or nestle between pages of a diary*

**STAKEOUT**
Hidden microphones are legally used to investigate serious crimes and threats to national security. Here, the head of security for a large American corporation listens in to a suspicious conversation. Laws limit the use of bugs, but some citizens' rights groups fear the controls are too weak.

*Compartments in spine of case conceal the power supply and transmitter electronics*

*Pocket calculator works normally, but broadcasts signal from sensitive microphone even while in use*

*Pen contains minute bug*

**MAKING A CASE FOR BUGGING**
Monitoring a meeting is a common task for both political and industrial spies. Business people can have many reasons for recording conversations: tapes can provide evidence of unfair competition, or help thwart a take-over by rivals. Bugging a briefcase is a discreet way to make a lasting record of "hush-hush" deals. Microphones built into an attaché case can pick up speech on the far side of a large room. The case can either record the conversation or transmit it to a monitoring device outside. Touching the lock and a brass rivet head at the same time activates the device. A bugged pen or calculator will attract no attention on a desk, and allow a spy to move the microphone nearer to the people talking.

# Dropping in

HOMING PIGEONS have played an important part in intelligence work since the earliest days of espionage. Carrying a precious cargo of vital secrets, a spy's airborne courier, the homing pigeon, can soar high over enemy territory. Roman general Julius Caesar (100–44 BC) used them to send intelligence messages during his campaigns in what is now France. Ever since, spies have valued the pigeon's speed and its ability to return home in almost any weather. More than half a million pigeons carried messages in World War I. Some even worked as spies – reconnaissance pigeons carried tiny cameras aloft to photograph enemy fortifications. In World War II, spies who located the launch sites of German "flying bombs" used pigeons to send the information to the Allied forces who bombed the sites.

*Lightweight, but strong, string attaches parachute to bird*

*Parachute made from cotton material*

*Miniature parachute canopy provided soft landing*

**PARACHUTING PIGEON**
Britain's SOE (pp. 32–33) dropped messenger pigeons to spies in occupied France by parachute. A special corselet protected the bird during descent. Agents collected the pigeons at the drop zone, and fed and cared for the birds until they were needed. This could be difficult as the pigeons required a lot of care and spies had to carry them with them if they went on long journeys. Some spies concealed the pigeons in deep pockets sewn into their waistcoats. When released from their temporary homes, the pigeons flew back to their lofts in England with secret messages in containers fixed to their legs.

*Lead weights were carefully placed so they did not rattle*

**SMUGGLING GOODS**
Airdrops supplied World War I spies with more than just pigeons to carry messages home. Money, weapons, and food all arrived by parachute, often cleverly disguised. This ox-tongue tin contains a map of France, a pair of wire cutters, and several compasses. Lead weights in the bottom of the tin prevented the tin from feeling unnaturally light.

*Message rolled inside cylinder*

**MESSAGE CANISTERS**
In both World Wars, pigeons carried secret messages in canisters. The French and German ones were made of lightweight aluminium, while British canisters were made of treated cardboard. The canisters were attached to the leg, and different colours indicated the intended destination of the message. For example, green was for coastal command and black for the SOE (pp. 32–33).

*String holds corselet round wings and tail feathers*

*Corselet made from linen and padded to protect bird*

*Hole in material for leg*

**MINUSCULE MESSAGE**
Pigeons could carry only light loads, so messages had to be small. This message, in German, from World War I, is written on a standard "pigeon post" form used by the German army. Longer messages could be microfilmed, even being reduced by photography to the size of a microdot (pp. 22–23) before being carried by messenger pigeon.

*Metal ring*

*Map printed on thin paper to fold up small inside tin*

*Corselet humanely kept the pigeon safe, yet restrained*

*Soldiers on the front line in World War II were ordered to shoot any bird they thought might be a carrier pigeon*

**DOUBLE DECKER**
During World War I pigeons travelled in style; dropped by parachute in a double-decker wicker basket. On landing, the basket's design allowed spies to carry it on their backs like a knapsack. Similar baskets used by American fighters in World War II had space for up to four birds and food.

*Wire fence cutters folded to fit in tin*

*Compass aided escaping spies*

*Lid and sides of basket were padded for extra protection*

*Birds travelled in suspended and padded corselets*

# Secret messages

SPIES RELY ON FAST, secure communications. Speed is crucial because intelligence quickly loses its value, and secrecy is essential to protect both the messages sent and the spy. The invention of radio at the beginning of this century improved the speed of such communications, but not the security. With radios, spies could communicate over long distances almost instantly. However, anyone tuning to the right wavelength was able to intercept radio messages. With two receivers and suitable antennae, counter-espionage agents could pinpoint the transmitter in a matter of minutes and capture the spy.

*Headphones allowed agent to listen to broadcasts without others hearing them*

*Oluf Reed Olsen's codesheets*

*Headphone connector*

*Frequency dial*

O. Reed Olsen.

KONFIDENTIELLT.
------------------------

INSTRUKSJONER

FOR BRUK AV

TYPE SS-TR 1 SENDE/MOTTAGERSETT.

N.B. LES DISSE INSTRUKSJONER GODT GJENNEM
FØR DU PRØVER AA BRUKE SETTET.

*Transmitter works from mains or battery power*

*Apparatus packs into a suitcase and weighs 14.5 kg (32 lb)*

*Voltage adjuster*

## HUMAN SIGNALS

Spies sometimes take desperate risks to carry intelligence. This World War I Belgian courier carried a message written on her back in invisible ink. Unfortunately, the ruse did not succeed: her captors discovered the message and executed the courier.

22

Spare valve

Crystal plugs in to change transmission frequency

Antenna – an 18-m (60-ft) length of wire – plugs in here

Terminals attached to car battery for transmission without mains power

Spare tubes were carried in this compartment

Tapping key sends coded messages as long and short pulses of radio waves

## NORWEGIAN SECRET AGENT

When German forces invaded neutral Norway in 1940, Oluf Reed Olsen fled the country in a sailing-boat. Reaching Britain, he trained as a radio operator, returning to Norway in 1943, where spies in the Kristiansand naval base supplied him with details of German shipping movements. Olsen coded the messages and transmitted them to Britain from a camouflaged camp hidden in the trees above the harbour at Kristiansand. He used the radio set shown here. The cipher was considered unbreakable because it was based on sets of random numbers of which Reed Olsen and MI6 held the only copies.

Oluf Reed Olsen using the Mark II suitcase radio at his camouflaged base in 1944

Message can be reduced until it is the size of a full stop

### MICRODOTS

Photography provides agents with a simple way to send messages secretly. By photographing a document with a special camera, a spy can produce a microdot – a negative that is 300 times smaller than the original. This paragraph about microdots can be reduced to a microdot the size of a full stop, and then hidden in a perfectly innocent letter. The agent who receives the letter can read every word of the microdot with the help of a microscope.

## CONVICTED BY RADIO

Peter and Helen Kroger hid a radio transmitter under the kitchen floor of their bungalow. With it they transmitted British submarine secrets to Russia. They chose a house in west London, England, close to three busy airports, hoping that communications between aircraft and control towers would hide their secret signals. At their trial in 1961, the radio was used as evidence.

## DOTTY PHOTOGRAPHY

Microdot cameras can be simple in construction, and small enough to hide easily. However, microphotography is difficult to do. Unless agents are very careful with the exposure of the film and its processing, the dot will be impossible to read.

Microdot camera (actual size)

## MICRODOTS

Photography provides agents with a simple way to send messages secretly. By photographing a document with a special camera, a spy can produce a microdot – a negative that is 300 times smaller than the original. This paragraph about microdots can be reduced to a microdot the size of a full stop, and then hidden in a perfectly innocent letter. The agent who receives the letter can read every word of the microdot with the help of a microscope.

# Codes and ciphers

ESPIONAGE AGENTS use "codes" to communicate, and "ciphers" to keep their messages secret. In a code, letters, numbers, or symbols replace the words of a message or signal. Some codes are in general use. For example, when you post a letter, a postcode guides it to the right destination. Spies sometimes send messages in Morse code – dots and dashes that all radio operators understand. Other codes are very complicated and difficult to break. Ciphers provide further secrecy. They are similar to codes but they have a secret "key" for encrypting the message – translating it into a cipher. The key can be a number, a word, even a poem. Anyone who has been given the key can easily decrypt the signal – change it back to plain text. Without knowing the key, the message reads as nonsense.

**SIMPLE CIPHER**
Ciphers do not need to be complicated if it is important only to hide their meaning from a casual glance. This jolly figure from World War I spells out "Ypres" (the site in France of a famous battle) and a date, the "8th".

**CIPHER DISC**
This metal cipher disc, invented in 1802, is less than 6 cm (2.5 in) in diameter. The two inner circles are rotated to align with different letters and numbers on the outer two circles. This produces a simple, easily-broken substitution cipher in which each letter stands for another, so "W", for example, represents "E" whenever it occurs.

*Codesheet is tiny so Yvonne Cormeau could easily hide it*

**CODESHEETS**
Charts like these make ciphers easy to write and hard to break. These miniature codesheets were hidden in the handbag of SOE wireless operator Yvonne Cormeau in World War II (pp. 32–33). When she used a chart for Morse transmissions, a different letter would replace "E" each time it occurred in the message.

*Moth's head conceals a fort on a knoll*

*Field gun*

*Machine-gun*

*Field gun*

*Fort is surrounded by entanglement*

*Enclosure for transport animals*

*Bridge*

*Broken ground*

*Stream*

*Machine-gun*

*Baden-Powell drew sketches of insects before he set out so he could adapt them easily when in the field*

**BUTTERFLY SKETCHES**
The eccentric English spy Robert Baden-Powell (1857–1941) disguised himself as a butterfly collector for one of his intelligence-gathering missions in Montenegro, on the coast of the Adriatic Sea. While he was there, he sketched this specimen of a moth perched on a twig.

**FORTRESS IN CIPHER**
In fact, Baden-Powell's drawing disguised a plan of the fortress at Kotor. Baden-Powell later taught espionage skills to the children in the Boy Scout movement that he founded in 1908.

## ROYAL CIPHER

Mary Queen of Scots (1542–87) encrypted messages to allies outside her prison walls (pp. 28–29). In the substitution cipher that they used, the same symbol stood for a letter each time it appeared, so that the cipher was easy to break.

*Coded letter signed by Anthony Babington, conspirator in a plot to assassinate Elizabeth I*

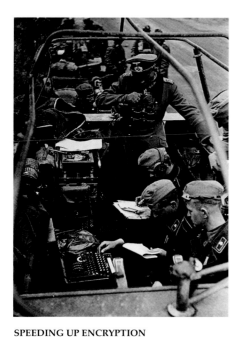

## SPEEDING UP ENCRYPTION

The Enigma cipher machine was used by German soldiers (above), diplomats, and spies in the 1930s and during World War II. The signals baffled enemy cryptanalysts (cipher experts) who intercepted them and tried to break the cipher. The Polish secret service, with the help of a recruited spy in the German cipher office, was able to interpret three-quarters of the Enigma messages by 1938, and in 1939, passed on this knowledge to Britain and France.

*Lid holds spare light bulbs*

*Numbers between the symbols represented people's names*

*Bulbs lit behind lettered windows on the lid to indicate enciphered character*

*Positions of rotors controlled encryption of each letter*

*Rotors spun after each letter, ensuring that cipher pattern never repeated*

*Cipher was keyed in*

*Connecting sockets with plugs made the cipher more complicated*

*Rotors and plugs gave several million million combinations*

## ENIGMA IN OPERATION

After setting plugs and three or four rotors, encryption on Enigma was automatic. Pressing a letter key lit up a different letter on the display above. The encrypted letter was different each time. Decryption on the receiving Enigma machine reversed the process. In principle, coded messages from the Enigma machine were impossible to read without knowing the rotor and plug settings. But that information and an actual Enigma machine supplied by the Polish Secret Service helped the British break most of the Enigma codes in an operation called "Ultra" which remained secret until 1972.

# Intercepts and code-breaking

**CIPHER CLERKS AT WORK**
Britain's code-breaking centre in World War II was at Bletchley Park near London. More than 5,000 staff there worked on up to 2,000 encrypted messages a day.

CIPHERS HELP PROTECT secret messages, but they do not destroy the meaning completely. Like a word puzzle, the sense of the message remains locked inside. An enemy who intercepts the signal will try hard to find the key. Intelligence agencies employ code-breakers called cryptanalysts to do this. With a substitution cipher (pp. 24–25), a cryptanalyst starts by counting letters. In English, "E" is used more often than other letters. So, if in the message "W" appears most, it probably stands for "E". The next step is to look for two-letter words ending in "E". There are only four in English: he, me, be, and we. Then the cryptanalyst will look for letters that stand on their own – in English there are just two one-letter words, "A" and "I". With techniques like these and even more complex ones, cryptanalysts can solve elaborate cipher puzzles, although it can sometimes take them a long time. Computers speed the process, but cryptanalysts need to be very patient. Few though, are as patient as a 17th-century Arab who deciphered a message to the Sultan of Morocco. It took him 16 years.

**ZIMMERMANN TELEGRAM**
Deciphered in Britain in 1916, this telegram was sent by the Germans to their ambassador in Mexico. It suggested that Mexico form an alliance with Germany and invade three southern US states. The interception of the telegram was possibly the most important spying event of the war. Shocked Americans quickly entered World War I on Britain's side.

*Polish inventors named machine after the ice-cream bombe they were eating at the time*

*WRENS (members of the Women's Royal Navy) operated the machines*

**GOING LIKE A BOMBE**
Cryptanalysts at the code-breaking centre at Bletchley Park used some of the first computers to help them break codes and ciphers. In two hours, a "bombe" could try every combination of rotor positions that was in use on the simple Enigma machines that Germany was using until 1938. A later machine called Colossus, was a forerunner of the programmable computers in use today.

*Bombe simply stopped when it broke the cipher*

*The attack was at night and US servicemen were asleep in their bunks*

*Unprepared US technicians thought the Japanese planes were part of a training exercise*

Japanese aircraft bomb Pearl Harbor, 7 December, 1941

## THE PURPLE MACHINE
Like Enigma (pp. 24–25), the Japanese Purple cipher machine used a plug board to create a huge number of possible keys. However, Purple used telephone switches in place of the rotors found in Enigma. A team of US cryptanalysts, including William Friedman (below left), cracked the Purple cipher by building a replica of the mechanism.

## PEARL HARBOR PREDICTED
By cracking the Purple code (right), American cipher experts predicted a Japanese attack on 7 December 1941, but could not name the hour or the place. The spies Richard Sorge (pp. 34–35) and Dusko Popov (pp. 56–57) had also warned of the air attack. American politicians decided to do nothing, and the devastating surprise raid took place on Pearl Harbor in Hawaii. The attack killed 2,300 Americans, as well as crippling the American fleet, and drawing the United States into World War II.

## HUSBAND AND WIFE TEAM
Russian-born American William F. Friedman (1891–1969) led the US Army Signals Intelligence Service team that cracked Japan's Purple cipher. Friedman worked on ciphers during both world wars. In the 1920s, his wife Elizebeth broke the codes of rum smugglers during prohibition, when alcohol was banned in the United States.

Herbert Yardley's security pass

## PIONEERING CRYPTANALYST
Herbert Osborne Yardley (1889–1958) was a brilliant cryptanalyst and pioneered code-breaking for the United States during World War I and afterwards. He set up the US unit that became known as the "Black Chamber" to read foreign intelligence material. His work in the 1920s was later used to help break the Purple cipher.

## THE "DEAD SOLDIER"
In 1943, the drowned body of a British major was washed ashore in Spain. Papers he was carrying described plans by the Allies to attack Greece and Sardinia, and German troops immediately moved there. In fact "Major Martin" was actually a civilian who had died of pneumonia. Intelligence chiefs had arranged for his body to be dressed as a soldier, and pushed from a submarine off the Spanish coast. The Germans were completely taken in, and when they moved their troops, they left very few soldiers on Sicily – the Allies' real target.

*Planted theatre ticket stubs made the major's story appear genuine*

"Major Martin's" fake identity card planted by intelligence officers

*Photograph of living person who looked like "Major Martin"*

# Concealment

A CLOAK AND DAGGER are the traditional trademarks of the secret agent. The spy hides the dagger, the badge of the assassin, under the cloak, which stands for secrecy, disguise, and concealment. Spies of the past could put on a cloak quickly to hide their true identity. Some chose more exotic disguises – Louis XV's agent the Chevalier d'Eon dressed as a woman for many years. For a modern spy, disguise is just as necessary, but much more subtle. Today's agents try to look ordinary, aiming to pass unnoticed in a crowd. Agents also choose ordinary-looking objects as hiding-places. Hidden in a working battery, a secret message is safe from even a close inspection. By miniaturizing their messages, spies can conceal them in even smaller objects. Large objects are more difficult to hide. But an ingenious and determined spy can hide heavy equipment, tank engines – even kidnapped people.

*Wrist strap*

*Right-angle viewfinder*

*Lens*

*Direct vision viewfinder*

*Setting for bright light*

*Aperture setting knob*

## ROYAL BEER BARREL
Imprisoned by England's Queen Elizabeth I, Mary, Queen of Scots (1542–87) smuggled messages to sympathizers in a beer barrel. She wrapped encrypted documents in a waterproof bag, probably an animal bladder. Then she pushed the bag through the bung hole into the barrel. Replies travelled back into her prison by the same route. Her "postman", a double agent called Gilbert Gifford, betrayed the scheme (pp. 42–43).

Mary, Queen of Scots

*Top hides 35 mm film*

## SMILE PLEASE!
"Detective" cameras disguised as books, hats and neck-ties first appeared in the 1880s. As early as 1893 spies were taking pictures with cameras shaped like pocket watches. This wrist-watch camera dates from 1948. On its 25-mm (1-inch) diameter disc of film it takes eight pictures, each the size of a little fingernail.

*Cell provides 1.5 volt power*

*Compartment is big enough to hold a roll of film*

*Magnet grips base to unscrew it*

*Wooden bung seals barrel when full of beer*

*Spike pushes into ground*

## DEAD LETTER DROP
Many spies conceal messages in prearranged hiding-places, or "dead drops". Leaving a message in a spike at a dead drop is safer than arranging to meet an agent.

## BATTERIES INCLUDED
This ingenious hiding-place looks like a normal battery, and a cell inside provides enough power to light a bulb. However, there is a secret compartment at the base.

Dukes as Comrade
Piotrovsky

Dukes as an ailing
intellectual

Dukes as a bearded
worker

Dukes as a sufferer from
epilepsy

Contemporary
print of the
Chevalier d'Eon

*D'Eon complained that
he sometimes forgot
whether he was wearing
a woman's headdress
or a man's helmet*

*People even
made bets on
d'Eon's true sex*

**A RELUCTANT WOMAN**
The Chevalier d'Eon (1728–
1810) was an expert fencer and
lawyer. He began his career as
a spy for French king Louis XV
in 1756. He posed as a shy
woman in the Russian court
to gain the confidence of
the Russian empress,
and also worked as
a double agent for
the British. He
lived in London
as a female at the
end of his life, and
when he died,
many people were
shocked to learn
his real identity.

**AGENT ST 25**
Paul Dukes became an expert
in disguise as head of British
intelligence in Russia. He was in
Moscow in 1917 when revolution
swept the communists to power.
Pursued by the Cheka (secret
police), Dukes cheekily
posed as a Comrade
Piotrovsky, a Cheka
officer. To the British,
he was "Agent ST 25".

*Clamps held
ankles and neck*

*Small seat*

**HOW TO SMUGGLE A SPY**
In 1964, drugged and bundled
in a trunk, Israeli Mordecai
Louk narrowly escaped being
exported from Rome to Cairo
disguised as "diplomatic
mail". He was freed when a
customs guard heard the
box whimper. Louk
had been spying
in Italy for the
Egyptians.

*Leather
slots for feet*

*Trunk was only
137 cm (53 in) long*

# Spies at war

ADVANCING ARMIES rely on expert soldiers to survey the land ahead, and judge the enemy's strength. However, not all are spies. Some are scouts who work openly, and wear army uniforms. If they are caught, they spend the rest of the war in prison. Wartime spies, though, disguise themselves to avoid capture, and they collect information secretly. So anyone caught in enemy territory wearing the clothes of a civilian can be tried as a spy, and the punishment – usually execution – is immediate. Despite this harsh penalty, spies have operated in almost every war. The 18th-century German king, Frederick the Great, even bragged about the number he employed. Mocking a French commander as a gourmet, he joked "A hundred cooks follow him – but ahead of me go a hundred spies!"

Major Coleridge's diary, 13 July 1899

### SOUTHERN BELLE
Many women worked as spies in the US Civil War (1861–65) and Belle Boyd (1844–1900) became one of the most famous Confederate (Southern) agents. She learned military secrets from Unionist (Northern) officers lodged in her Virginia home, and braved gunfire to tell Confederate leaders. After capture and then release in a prisoner exchange, she received a heroine's welcome in the South.

### DEATH OF A SPY
Major John André (1751–80) was hanged as a spy during the American Revolution (1775–83). He had gone to meet US traitor Benedict Arnold (1741–1801), the commander of West Point, a fortress which guarded the Hudson River Valley. Arnold wanted to surrender the fort to the British, and he handed André details of his plans. The ship that was to take André and the secret plans back to the British Army was fired on and left without him. André disguised himself as a civilian, but was caught by the American militia with the secret papers hidden in his boots. The British spy was hanged in 1780.

### DETECTIVE SPYMASTER
When civil war divided the United States, Abraham Lincoln turned to a private detective to help gather intelligence for the Unionist army. The choice seemed to be a natural one – the Scotsman Allan Pinkerton (1819–84), head of the famous detective agency, had already foiled one attempt to assassinate President Lincoln. Unfortunately, Pinkerton knew very little about war, and his agents were often clumsy and sometimes cowardly. He resigned as Lincoln's spymaster in 1862.

*Hollow bullet used by Major Coleridge to hide his messages*

## FIGHTING THE BOERS
In the Boer War (1899–1902) British forces fought to control farms and gold in what is now South Africa. Their enemies the Afrikaners, or Boers, were descendants of white Dutch settlers. Major H. F. Coleridge was among those who spied for the British, and his diaries (left) record details of the Boer defences. The British intelligence service did not realize the value of the intelligence that spies like Coleridge supplied, and he had to plead for more money to continue his work (below).

### CARTOON CAPTURE
During World War I (1914–18), spies usually operated far from the front line, in neutral nations such as Switzerland and the Netherlands (Holland). Nevertheless, the public fear of spies and their exploits inspired many cartoons. This colourful example shows a German spy captured by French troops.

*Coleridge sent this telegram asking for more money in 1900*

*French-born Violette Szabo was the best shot in Britain's SOE*

*Lincoln (centre) also dismissed his general*

*On 17 September 1862, 12,000 Unionist troops died at the battle of Antietam, largely due to bad intelligence, and Pinkerton resigned*

### COURAGEOUS COMMANDO
Violette Szabo's only qualification when she applied to be a British spy in World War II (1939–45) was her skill with a rifle – London shooting galleries banned her because she always hit the target. She became a spy to avenge the death of her husband Etienne (above), who died fighting for the British in north Africa, and was admired by fellow spies for her courage and determination. She was captured after a gun battle on her second SOE (Special Operations Executive) mission in France, when she was sabotaging telegraph lines. Violette Szabo was executed in a German prison camp.

### TOO GOOD TO BE TRUE
The cleverest agent of World War II, codenamed "Cicero", was extremely good at spying for Germany. He was an Albanian and his real name was Elyesa Bazna. While working as valet to the British ambassador in Turkey, he opened the embassy safe, and photographed secret codes, lists of British spies, and the Allied plans to invade Europe. But these documents were so secret that the German leaders could not believe they were genuine, and ignored Cicero. Nevertheless, they paid him a fortune in banknotes – but all of them were forgeries.

# A cover story

**BITTER PILL**
All SOE agents carried a suicide L-pill which would kill in five seconds. No agent ever used it.

$D$ISGUISED AS A CHILD'S NURSE, "Annette" passes through a wartime roadblock in south-west France. "Annette", who is really the radio operator Yvonne Cormeau, tells her "cover story" well, escaping capture for a year, and transmitting over 400 coded messages. During World War II, the lives of many secret agents depended on their cover stories – invented pasts designed to hide their real identity. In Britain, the Special Operations Executive (SOE) trained agents, giving them cover stories that they learned by heart. Then the SOE dropped the agents in France by parachute or small boat.

Fake French matchbox

**FOR DEFENCE**
Male and female agents learned techniques of silent killing, and all carried knives to put the techniques into practice if necessary.

**VITAL TIMING**
A late arrival usually signalled danger. Cautious agents did not wait more than a few minutes at a rendezvous.

**PARTING GIFT**
SOE agents were given a valuable present such as this silver cigarette case before leaving on a mission. The gift could be used as a bribe if an agent was caught by a corrupt official.

**MAPS**
War agents used maps to plan sabotage. A silk map (above) folds very small to aid concealment.

*Wallet*

*Powder compact*

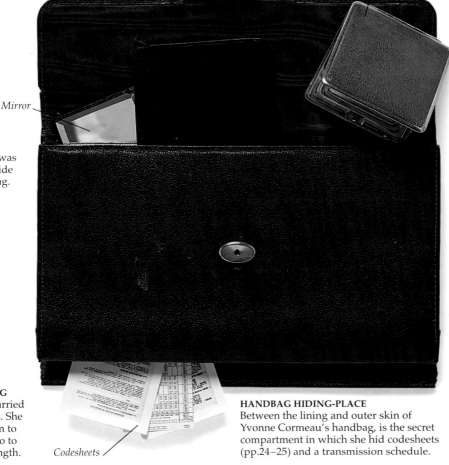

*Mirror*

**TINY TAPPER**
A Morse code key was small enough to hide easily in a handbag.

**PLUG IN TUNING**
Yvonne Cormeau carried a variety of crystals. She could change them to tune her SOE radio to the correct wavelength.

*Codesheets*

**HANDBAG HIDING-PLACE**
Between the lining and outer skin of Yvonne Cormeau's handbag, is the secret compartment in which she hid codesheets (pp.24–25) and a transmission schedule.

The clothes had to be tailored in the French style of the 1940s

SOE carefully removed all English labels before sending an agent into enemy territory

Every detail of clothing reinforced the cover story – an agent posing as a clerk would wear a simple, inexpensive hat like this one

Yvonne Cormeau's battered leather briefcase

Briefcase fitted in with one of Yvonne Cormeau's disguises – a district nurse

**YVONNE CORMEAU, SOE RADIO OPERATOR**
Many of these items belonged to Yvonne Cormeau, the SOE agent whose cover name was "Annette". She parachuted in to France on the night of 22–23 August 1943, and worked as a radio operator. Her natural caution helped her to avoid being captured until Allied forces liberated France in 1944. On one occasion, she recognized another agent on a train but resisted the temptation to speak – she had learned in training that if he was under suspicion, they might both be captured. On the other hand, Yvonne Cormeau knew when it was worth taking a risk. Although most radio operators moved their radio sets daily to avoid capture, she felt safe transmitting from the same house for six months. From the windows she could spot interception vans over 5 km (3 miles) away.

Stockings could be used as a bribe by the SOE agent as silk was very rare in wartime

Yvonne Cormeau's dress was made from lightweight cotton

Suede shoes

33

# Double agents and defectors

**A TRAITOR'S DEATH**
Japanese counter-espionage agents unmasked Richard Sorge for their German allies. He was condemned and executed in 1944.

**TRIBUTE TO A SPY**
Richard Sorge (1895–1944) appeared to be a fanatical Nazi during World War II. While a political adviser to the German ambassador, he was feeding secrets to Germany's Russian enemies. Soviet stamps showed Sorge as a hero.

DOUBLE AGENTS ARE REALLY "controlled enemy agents". Rather than serving two masters they work for only one side in a war of espionage – but they deceive the other side into thinking they are working for them and instead steal their secrets. Being a double agent is very risky. To be successful they must develop the trust of an intelligence agency, while their sole aim is to betray that trust. If caught they can expect no mercy in their punishment. Double agents may be volunteers, or they could be spies unmasked by counter-intelligence agencies who have been "turned" (recruited and controlled) rather than prosecuted. Spies who are turned are especially valuable. Their new masters provide them with false but believable information, and the spy passes on the bogus secrets as if they were true. Spies that flee to the nation that was once the target of their espionage are called "defectors". Although they may be admired in the country to which they are truly loyal, they earn just as much hatred in the country they betrayed.

Aldrich and Rosario Ames after their separate trials for spying

**RUSSIAN AGENT AT THE CIA**
For nine years Aldrich Ames (born 1941) was a Soviet spy while working as a trusted officer at the CIA. Ames and his wife Rosario provided details of many spies recruited by the CIA and, with their help, Moscow was able to build a network of double agents who deceived their CIA bosses. The pair were paid well by the Russians for their treachery.

**ANCIENT SPYMASTER**
Chinese commander Sun Tzu was among the first to write about double agents. He called them, "doomed spies", who "are deliberately given false information and told to report it to the enemy." Sun Tzu wrote his book, *The Art of War*, in the 4th century BC.

# ЗДРАВСТВУЙТЕ, ТОВАРИЩ ФИЛБИ

«Если бы мне предстояло начать жизнь сызнова, я начал бы так, как начал».

**Феликс ДЗЕРЖИНСКИЙ.**

ДЕКАБРЬСКОЕ морозное утро, ночная мгла еще не ушла с заснеженных улиц. Деревья на Гоголевском бульваре покрыты пушистым инеем. У троллейбусной остановки — цепочка по-

представить все, что угодно. Предположить, что я в августовское утро в халате за столом напротив него сидел кадровый сотрудник советской разведки, он не мог даже в дурном сне.

— Каким же образом, товарищ Ким, вам удалось попасть на службу в английскую разведку?
— Это довольно длинная история, — говорит он. — После окончания Кэмбриджа я некоторое время работал в одной

— Я делал, что мог в то время, и был зачислен в кадры советской разведки.

— Я пошел вверх по служебной лестнице. Через год я уже был заместителем начальника одного из отделов МИ-6.
— МИ-6, что это значит?
— В Англии существует две службы: под кодовым названием МИ-5 скрывается контрразведка, МИ-6 — это собственно секретная разведывательная служба.
— Западная пресса отмечала, что ва-

Он был внимателен в обращении с людьми, но по существу относился к ним свысока. В дела он не вникал, и, я бы сказал, при всей его агрессивности он был дилетантом, о чем лучше всего говорит авантюра с вторжением на Кубу. Считают, что он занял этот пост благодаря своему брату — Джону Фостеру Даллесу

**COLD WAR DOUBLE AGENT**
Harold "Kim" Philby (1912–88) became a communist while he was studying at Cambridge University, and was a Soviet spy by 1933. Yet, seven years later, he had a job with Britain's MI6 intelligence service. After thirty years of spying he fled to Moscow. A grateful Soviet Union gave him a pension and a flat, the office of which is shown above.

**HERO'S WELCOME**
Philby escaped to Moscow from Beirut, where he had been working under cover as a journalist. The Soviet newspapers welcomed him with banner headlines. This one reads "Greetings Comrade Philby."

*Hammer and sickle, the symbol of the Soviet Union*

**RETIREMENT IN MOSCOW**
After defecting, Philby lived in Moscow until his death in 1988. His son took this photograph of him in the 1970s. The treachery of Philby and his fellow spies Guy Burgess and Donald Maclean left behind a trail of mistrust. Their espionage discredited the British intelligence services.

**MEDALS FROM BOTH SIDES**
Philby received this KGB badge soon after his arrival in Moscow. Later the Soviet Union awarded him the Order of the Red Banner. Eighteen years before, England's King George VI, unaware that he was a spy, had given Kim the Order of the British Empire.

**SECURITY SECRETS**
As head of the KGB mission in London, Oleg Gordievsky (born 1939) had access to the most sensitive information about his country's espionage. Yet secretly he despised the Soviet system, and had been spying for the West since 1966. He defected to Britain in 1985 when his Soviet masters began to suspect him.

*Gordievsky wrote memoirs of his time in the KGB*

**SECRET IDENTITY**
Igor Gouzenko (1919–82) was a cipher clerk in the Soviet Embassy in Ottawa. He did not wish to return to the Soviet Union, and defected with evidence of Soviet spying. He was turned away as a crank by newspapers and government departments, but the Mounted Police believed and protected him. For this TV interview he wore a hood to keep his identity secret.

*Gordievsky with his book KGB: The Inside Story*

35

# Secret weapons

ESPIONAGE HAS A BLOODY PAST. Spies were busiest in wartime, when there was danger everywhere, and when war ended it was the job of intelligence organizations to make sure peace continued. Sometimes they used weapons to achieve this peaceful aim, and many wartime spies carried weapons openly. Others disguised their guns and knives in often ingenious ways. With the Cold War (pp. 38–39) came greater secrecy. Both Warsaw Pact and Western powers attempted killings, and some, such as the murder of Georgi Markov, succeeded. Other schemes did not: the CIA twice tried, and failed, to kill Cuba's president Fidel Castro (pp. 42–43) with poison. The agency also considered more unusual weapons. They plotted to put deadly bacteria in Castro's cigar, and to blow him up with an exploding clam while he swam in the sea. But not all the agency's weapons would have been fatal. The strangest plot aimed to humiliate Castro. By putting special powder in the communist leader's shoes, CIA agents planned to make his distinctive beard fall out!

*Pushing the trigger near the handle fired the pellet*

**DEADLY PENCIL**
Disguised as pencils, these two weapons were used in close combat. The stabbing pencil contains a cross-shaped blade, and the propelling pencil fired a single chromium-plated bullet. Agents of Britain's SOE (pp. 32–33) used them to gain a brief advantage, so that they could seize more powerful weapons from their opponents.

*Pencil is cut away here to show knife inside*

*Gun has no barrel, limiting accuracy*

*Shortened barrel*

Modified Webley & Scott 6.35 mm pistol

Georgi Markov in 1978

**UMBRELLA KILLER**
The Bulgarian Georgi Markov broadcast, from the BBC in London, criticism of his country's leadership. Walking home along a London street one day in 1978, Markov felt a sharp pain. He looked round to see a man picking up an umbrella. Markov developed a fever, and died three days later. His assassin, a Bulgarian agent, had used a specially designed umbrella to fire a tiny pellet containing a powerful poison into Markov. Ten days earlier Bulgarian agents in Paris had attacked another opponent of the country's rulers, but the victim recovered.

*Gas cylinder made umbrella work like air rifle*

*Holes in tiny pellet contained poison*

*Trigger guard*

**GUN BELT**
Worn on a belt under clothing, this small World War II pistol had a very short range. To be sure of a direct hit an assassin needed to be standing right next to the target. A firing cable from the buckle passed down the sleeve of the coat that covered the gun. The great advantage was that a spy could pull the trigger without anyone seeing him or her aim or fire.

## SIMPLE SLASHERS
Not all weapons were aimed at people. These razor-sharp knives were designed to destroy vehicle tyres. They were small enough to hide easily, yet with a single slash an agent could gain valuable minutes in which to make an escape. Saboteurs used the knives to completely immobilize a vehicle by slashing all the tyres (including the spare).

*Knife hung from thong around neck*

*Small slasher resembles ring*

## RING REVOLVER
Concealed weapons are nothing new. The well-equipped French spy of the 19th century carried this tiny revolver fixed to a ring. By revolving the chamber the agent could fire five shots. Because of its small size and firing method this design was sometimes called a squeezer pistol or palm pistol.

*Because the pistol is so small, it had a very limited range*

*The ring gun can fire five bullets*

## LETHAL GLOVE
Some weapons used by spies appear more dangerous to the person using them than to the victim. An agent firing this ingenious glove pistol had to take careful aim as there was only one bullet and that could easily take off a couple of fingers. The United States Office of Naval Intelligence produced the gun for its World War II agents.

*Barrel poked out between fingers*

*Pistol is riveted to a leather glove*

*Pressing the barrel against the victim's body fired the gun*

*Canadian maple leaf*

*Concealed blade*

*Concealed blade*

*French tricolour*

## HEEL AND COIN BLADES
Despite their vicious appearance, knives hidden in shoe heels were not intended for attack. Instead the concealed blades allowed agents who were tied up to cut themselves free. Spies also hid knives in low denomination coins. They hoped that their guards would let them keep the loose change in their pockets – even if the guards stole the banknotes.

*Coin has a hidden blade*

## MESSY KNIVES
Wartime intelligence agencies designed these small knives so they could be hidden in a coat lapel or cuff. A captured agent could use the knife to attack guards and escape. Instructors who trained the spies warned that the results were often "messy".

# The Cold War

Wᴇɴ ᴡᴏʀʟᴅ ᴡᴀʀ ɪɪ ᴇɴᴅᴇᴅ in 1945, the future looked bleak for secret agents. In fact, a golden age of espionage was about to begin. A political boundary split Europe in two. Nicknamed the "Iron Curtain", it was actually just a line on a map. To the east lay the communist world – the Soviet Union and its allies – who wanted to create a classless society that shared everything. Nations to the west, supported by the United States, were capitalist, believing in the private ownership of property and businesses. Eastern and Western nations were deeply suspicious of each other, and their intense rivalry became known as the Cold War. Spies thrived in the atmosphere of mistrust that the Cold War created. They had plenty of work, with East and West racing each other to build the biggest bombs, and each side sending spies to discover what the other side was plotting. And because of all this activity, each side needed more spies at home to catch enemy agents at work. On both sides of the Iron Curtain, fear of nuclear war meant that the money for spying never ran out. Finally, in 1989, the Cold War ended and the process of reuniting Germany, which had also been split in two, began.

**HUNT THE MISSILE**
Missile bases are easy to spot on photographs from spy satellites (pp. 52–53), so the United States and the Soviet Union developed submarine-based missile launchers which could hide beneath the waves. The designers of this Trident missile claimed it would be used to hit missile bunkers. Opponents believed that cities would be the real targets.

*Distinctive mushroom-shaped cloud*

**TESTING THE BOMB**
The United States tested its atom bombs in the Nevada desert, far from the prying eyes of enemy spies. The power of these bombs to destroy civilization frightened everyone, and may have gone a long way towards ensuring that neither side in the Cold War actually used one.

*Crowds cheered as everyone with a hammer and chisel chipped at the wall*

**"KEEPING THE WORLD SAFE"**
Politicians in the Cold War believed in "mutually assured destruction" (MAD). If each side had enough bombs to destroy the other, they reasoned, neither side would dare risk war. The two "superpowers", the Soviet Union and the United States, each built huge missiles with nuclear warheads. They never launched them, and these American Titan II missiles are in storage, waiting to be converted into satellite launchers.

**THE WALL DIVIDING EUROPE**
Cold War espionage was most intense in Berlin, the capital of East Germany. Berlin was situated well inside East Germany, but a wartime treaty gave France, Britain, and the United States control of West Berlin, so the city was itself divided into East and West. To prevent refugees escaping to the West across the new border, the East Germans divided the city of Berlin by building a wall in 1961. The wall's destruction by the people in 1989 united Germany, and symbolized the end of the Cold War.

## EUROPE DIVIDED

In the Cold War, only four European nations were neutral. Most others signed pacts vowing to defend their neighbours. The Warsaw Pact united communist countries with the Soviet Union. Capitalist countries were allied with the United States as members of the North Atlantic Treaty Organization (NATO).

## BERLIN SPY SWAP

Any captured Cold War spies could expect execution or, at best, a long spell in jail – unless their government could negotiate a prisoner exchange. Under these deals, East and West swapped captured spies. The released agents walked to freedom at one of the checkpoints along the Berlin Wall.

## SHOT DOWN

Before satellites simplified spying from above the ground, the United States sent U-2 spy planes (pp. 52–53) to photograph the other side of the Iron Curtain. The Soviet Union shot one down in 1960, and captured the CIA spy pilot, Gary Powers. He did not have to serve the ten-year sentence because the Soviets freed him in 1962 in exchange for Soviet spy Rudolph Abel.

U-2 pilot Gary Powers pictured after being shot down in 1960

Iron Curtain

Neutral countries

Other capitalist nations

Full NATO members

Other communist nations

Warsaw Pact countries

Soviet Union

*Graffiti added to remains of wall after reunification*

# Spymasters

ESPIONAGE CHIEFS HAVE enormous influence. The secrecy that surrounds all intelligence work means that, although most chiefs serve their country wisely, those that choose not to have dangerous powers. Usually spymasters take orders from a trusted group inside a country's ruling party, but often members of that party do not know what the spies are really doing. In the past, spymasters received their orders directly from the king or queen. However, in 1519 a Venetian diplomat wrote of the English King Henry VIII's first spymaster Cardinal Wolsey that he "...rules both king and the entire kingdom". In this century, until the Cold War ended, secret service chiefs controlled whole Eastern European nations. J. Edgar Hoover's powers grew so great whilst he was the FBI chief, that he was in a position to blackmail some of the most influential politicians in the United States. Countries are now more open about the existence of their security services, but the identity of agents in the spy networks is still a closely guarded secret.

**ROMAN SOLDIER**
General Scipio Africanus Major (236 BC – 184 BC) was among the most clever spymasters of the Roman Empire. While attacking the Spanish city of Carthago Nova, his spies discovered that the enemy's reinforcements were ten days' march away. As a result, the navy and army under Scipio's leadership won an easy victory.

**POWER BEHIND THE THRONE**
Cardinal Wolsey (1475–1530) became the most powerful man in England as the first head of intelligence services for King Henry VIII. Wolsey's agents opened the mail sent to diplomats from Venice and other nations. To protect their secrets, the ambassadors began to write their letters in code. Thomas Cromwell took over from Wolsey as controller.

Wolsey had influence over the English king Henry VIII for many years

**INDIAN INTELLIGENCE**
Mughal ruler Akbar (1542–1605) united India. As a young king, he used fakirs (holy men) as spies. During his reign (1556–1605), Akbar extended the Indian empire, reforming the government. To do this he also relied on intelligence reports provided by *kotwal* (local officials), who had a duty to employ spies.

**INVISIBLE SPIES**
The warring princes of 12th-century Japan used *ninja* as spies and silent assassins. The ninja got their name from the Japanese word meaning "to make yourself invisible". They were trained to high standards of fitness, and were masters of disguise. One warlord, Takeda Shingen, so feared them that he fitted a second door to his lavatory to make escape easier.

**RUSSIAN SECRET SERVICE**
The first Tsar of Russia, Ivan IV (1530–1584) richly deserved his nickname "The Terrible". He ruled with the help of ruthless secret agents called the *Oprichniki*. Officially security police, the Oprichniki were really thugs who terrorized whole communities, killing and torturing without fear of punishment. They wore an emblem of a dog's head and a broom, symbolizing their powers to sniff out and sweep away treason.

**FATHER OF THE SECRET SERVICE**
Francis Walsingham (c. 1532–1590) did much to build up the English intelligence service. His greatest achievement was to uncover a plot to murder England's queen, Elizabeth I. Walsingham's agents intercepted coded letters between the plotters and the queen's imprisoned cousin Mary, Queen of Scots. The letters proved that Mary was involved, and she was executed in February 1587.

*Walsingham's cipher agents forged an extra paragraph asking Mary for the plotters' names*

*The letter was written in a simple code*

**THE RED CARDINAL**
Cardinal Richelieu (1585–1642) organized the Cabinet Noir, a secret police force in France. His men spied on noble families, giving Louis XIII more power. The spies gained a reputation – every French teacher of sword-fighting was thought to be an agent.

**A NEW BROOM SWEEPS CLEAN**
For nearly half a century, J. Edgar Hoover (1895–1972) was the head of the FBI, one of the functions of which was to detect enemy spies at work in the United States. But Hoover's agents also snooped on the private lives of politicians, even the president himself. By threatening to make sordid secrets public, Hoover clung to his huge power. In 1947, the CIA was formed to deal with foreign security, and the power of the FBI was curbed.

**WOLF IN SHEEP'S CLOTHING**
"The man without a face" was Markus Wolf's nickname during the Cold War. He was in charge of foreign operations for East Germany's Stasi (secret police). Wolf managed highly effective spy rings in the West. Even one of the close aides of the West German chancellor, Willy Brandt (b.1913), had been recruited and was a Stasi spy.

**DOUBLE AGENT AT THE TOP**
Alfred Redl (1846–1913) was Austria's chief spycatcher. He modernized the Austrian Secret Service but ran up huge personal debts. When Russia offered him money for vital information, he accepted, and worked with them for ten years. Redl was accused of being a traitor in 1913, and shot himself rather than stand trial.

# The secret services

BEHIND EVERY SPY is a vast network for gathering intelligence. Organizations like the CIA and MI6 give spies documents, money, and help, and interpret the intelligence that the spies collect. The intelligence networks analyze information not only from human spies, but also from a host of other sources. Satellites provide some of their data and interception of radio signals supplies more. Many of their staff do nothing but read foreign newspapers, magazines, and journals. A clever analyst can learn much from these "open sources". During World War II, Russian intelligence experts noticed the United States was hoarding silver for "scientific research", and had banned all atomic physics journals. Without putting agents' lives at risk, they guessed – correctly – that the United States was developing an atom bomb.

## SPY VS SPY
*Mad* magazine's cartoon figures made fun of secret service rivalry at the height of the Cold War.

Message reads: "At all times protect (our) secrets (and) everywhere guard against spies"

## BEWARE OF SPIES
The Republic of China has a large but highly secretive intelligence network. There is a Central Control of Intelligence that collects information, relying on different government organizations as well as the ordinary person in the street. In the 1970s, plaques such as this one (left) were posted all over the country to warn citizens against the activities of spies. Outside China, spies are believed to operate through the country's embassies and the New China News Agency.

The emblem of the CIA

## GUARDIANS OF THE UNITED STATES
The Central Intelligence Agency (CIA) has collected and analyzed foreign intelligence for the United States since 1947. It is also responsible for counter-intelligence abroad. The less well-known National Security Agency, which is under the control of the Federal Bureau of Investigation (FBI), is actually bigger than the CIA, and handles signal intelligence – codes, ciphers, and the interception of communications. A separate organization, the United States Secret Service, has responsibility for protecting the president.

Badge of MI5, the counter-espionage agency in Britain

## THE STASI
Until Germany's two halves were reunited in 1990, the Stasi (State Security) controlled espionage for the East. East Germans had good reason to fear these secret police. The Stasi employed more than 85,000 people and had detailed files on a third of the East German population.

Copy camera with Stasi insignia

## SECURITY STAR
Britain has twin security agencies to handle intelligence and counter-intelligence at home (MI5) and abroad (MI6). In 1992, Britain was the first country to appoint a woman, Stella Rimington, as the head of a major intelligence agency. Until 1995, she was director of MI5, also called the Security Service, and originally formed in 1906. MI6 is the military name for the Secret Intelligence Service, and staff refer to its shadowy director as "C".

Badge worn by
a KGB agent

*Map showing
the Soviet Union*

## ISRAELIS SPYING ABROAD
Israel has developed ruthlessly efficient security and intelligence services. Formed in 1949, Mossad (the Institution for Intelligence and Special Services) is responsible for foreign espionage and taking action against the country's enemies. Shin Beth (Security and Counter-espionage Service) handles internal security.

*A menorah – the symbol of Judaism*

Badge of Mossad

*Vanunu's desperate message about his kidnapping in Rome*

## MOSSAD AT WORK
Agents of Mossad are particularly skilled at undercover work in foreign countries. When Mordechai Vanunu, a senior nuclear technician, revealed that Israel was building atom bombs, Mossad agents kidnapped him in Italy and took him back to Israel to face trial and imprisonment. When in Israeli custody, Vanunu wrote a message for the press on his hand, giving details of the kidnapping.

## SPYING IN RUSSIA
The KGB (Committee of State Security) controlled the intelligence and counter-intelligence agencies both inside the Soviet Union and overseas from 1954 until the 1980s. KGB agents also handled internal security, and the head of the organization had great political influence. With the birth of modern Russia, the duties of the KGB were transferred to less powerful organizations in the new republics.

Manurhin
7.65 mm
pistol

## TARGET PRACTICE
The secret intelligence organizations of all countries deny that their agents carry out political killings. However, history proves this is not true. The CIA was famous for the actions it took against foreign leaders who opposed the United States – they hired Mafia killers to try and assassinate Cuba's communist president, Fidel Castro (pp. 36–37). And the KGB defector Oleg Gordievsky claims that the KGB provided the poisoned umbrella that killed Georgi Markov (pp. 36–37).

## PROTECTING FRANCE
Like many other nations, France divides its intelligence work among several organizations. The Direction Générale de la Sécurité Extérieure (DGSE) collects foreign intelligence and organizes counter-intelligence abroad. The efficient Direction de la Surveillance du Territoire (DST) is controlled by the Ministry of the Interior and handles internal security. In the early 1980s, the DST was directly responsible for the expulsion of 47 Soviet diplomats suspected of spying.

*DGSE agents abroad defend themselves with automatics like this*

# Surveillance at work

Sᴘɪᴇꜱ ᴄᴏᴜʟᴅ ʙᴇ ᴡᴀᴛᴄʜɪɴɢ ʏᴏᴜ. Business secrets are potentially valuable to rival companies, and to obtain those secrets, subterfuge is often used by employees or outside agencies. To steal documents, industrial spies use the tools and methods of a secret agent, and to protect the same documents from snoopers, businesses must adopt counter-espionage tactics (pp. 48–49). The devices shown here all help protect office secrets from intruders. However, all of them can also monitor employees, for the espionage threat may come from inside the company. Workplace spies can watch low-paid staff who may be bribed to sell information to rivals. The spies aim to catch disgruntled managers wiping computer discs. Even office gossip can be a target for hidden microphones: it may warn that senior staff plan to leave and set up in competition.

**ARE YOU RECEIVING ME?**
Business people can learn a lot about their clients with a tiny bug like this. A sales representative making a presentation can "accidentally" leave a bugged folder in the conference room to record a client's private conversation.

**TAKING PICTURES**
Professional spies might use an expensive camera like this Minox to copy information. However, the office photocopier is more of a security threat. Employees do not arouse suspicion when they use it – and the copies cost them nothing.

**BUGGING THE WORKPLACE**
An office appliance such as a fluorescent desk lamp is an ideal hiding-place for bugs (above). It has a built-in power supply and sits in the middle of the desk, so it is well placed to pick up any conversations. Bribing someone to insert the bug when equipment is sold is less risky than entering the office to plant it.

*Base of lamp is large enough to conceal bug*

*With a cheap modem, spies can hack into insecure computer networks and copy data files*

97% 63% 78% 49% 91%

**LOUD AND CLEAR**
A sales representative who has planted a bug is able to eavesdrop on his client from a car parked outside. By pulling up the radio antenna. he can pick up the signal and listen to any discussion of the sales pitch. The following day, the sales rep can return to negotiations, able to use the information to change strategy, and in a better position to bargain.

*Shredded paper*

**PINHOLE PEEPER**
More than one in every ten American companies use video cameras to spy on their employees. Concealing the cameras is simple: the smallest have lenses that are much smaller than a match-head.

**CAUGHT ON CAMERA**
FBI agents used a hidden video camera in 1979 to collect evidence in a corruption case that they nicknamed "ABSCAM". The video (above) proved that members of Congress (the United States parliament) were taking bribes. Seven members of Congress were convicted and went to jail.

**INFINITY RECEIVER**
Most office bugs have a limited range but infinity receivers use the telephone lines to allow eavesdropping from anywhere in the world that there is a telephone. The "spy" must first install the device, usually attached to the telephone line. The bug does not operate until the spy dials the number of the bugged telephone, followed by a specially-selected key on a touch-tone telephone. The bug detects the tone, and stops the target phone from ringing. Then it allows the spy to hear a conversation in the room, using the telephone mouthpiece as a microphone. With the infinity receiver, it is possible for someone in Sydney, Australia, to eavesdrop on conversations in Washington DC.

*Screwheads on clock can conceal camera*

*Tiny transmitters can be hidden anywhere – even in potted plants*

*An innocent desk accessory can easily hide a bug*

**TALKING RUBBISH**
Cutting up documents does not necessarily destroy them. Determined industrial spies can painstakingly piece together shredded secrets.

**BUG IN A PLUG**
Disguised as a wall socket, a bug is impossible to detect without taking the socket apart or using special equipment. The socket functions normally, and also supplies the bug with power. Some devices work like baby alarms, using the mains power cables – instead of radio waves – to transmit signals. The spy monitors any conversations with a suitable receiver plugged into any other socket on the same circuit.

*Infinity tape store (above) records phone calls and plays them back when the "spy" dials in*

# Industrial espionage

GOVERNMENTS AND POLITICIANS are not the only targets of espionage. Businesses also have secrets which industrial spies try to steal or copy. This kind of espionage is rapidly expanding, but it is hardly new. The silk industry was an early victim. Until the 6th century, only the Chinese knew how to make this luxurious cloth. Then the Byzantine emperor Justinian I (483–565) used espionage to steal the secret of its production. He encouraged two monks to smuggle silkworms out of China in hollow canes. Industrial spying is more sophisticated today, but governments still encourage it if their nation benefits. In 1989, the French Department of Commerce planned to steal trade secrets from American and British companies. The spying became public when an informer posted their "shopping list" to the CIA. Usually, though, it is businesses that use industrial espionage against their competitors. Successful spies find design details, lists of suppliers and buyers. Even advance knowledge of a price list can help squeeze a competitor out of business.

**SPYING ON THE COMPETITION**
One of the most common forms of industrial espionage is for trusted employees to quit and join a competitor – taking secrets with them. General Motors (GM) suspected José Ignacio Lopez de Arriortua of doing this when he left to join rivals Volkswagen. GM claimed that de Arriortua and other executives stole thousands of photographs and plans of the Opel Vectra which was then secret. The car is now on the market.

*Computer-aided designs of new cars are fiercely protected from industrial espionage*

General Motors' Opel Vectra

*In Europe, annual losses in audio, software, and video piracy are $6,003 million*

*Long before they emerge on the catwalk, designs of evening dresses are the target of spies*

## THE ENTERTAINMENT INDUSTRY

Piracy (illegal copying) and industrial espionage cut the profits made by people in the world of entertainment. From a single original, pirates can make millions of CDs or videos. Security at recording and film studios must be intense to make sure that master tapes are protected until the scheduled release date. Despite these precautions, industrial spies occasionally succeed in smuggling out a recording: pirates in Singapore made thousands of video copies of the James Bond film *A View to a Kill* and distributed them throughout Asia before the film's London première.

*To keep shape of new car secret, it can be disguised by fitting new parts in old car bodies when road-testing*

*Revolutionary disc braking systems may interest rival car manufacturers*

## COSTUME DRAMA

Theft of ideas and designs in the fashion industry is big business. It is easy to claim and often difficult to prove. Cutters and other workers in the garment trade might copy patterns and sell them to another designer. It is also possible to recreate designs from sketches or photographs taken at designer dress shows.

## INDUSTRIAL DIAMONDS

An industrial spy at General Electric earned $1 million a year for passing secrets of synthetic diamond manufacture to a South Korean company. By stealing the knowledge they needed to build the plant, the Koreans avoided paying licence fees for the technology, and in addition saved the enormous expense of funding a research and development programme. General Electric discovered the espionage in 1992.

*Tiny synthetic diamonds in drill's tip help it cut faster*

## COMPUTER SPYING

In 1981, the FBI caught a computer engineer, Kenji Hayashi, with secret details of IBM computer disk drive technology. His employers, Japan's Hitachi corporation, gave him more than half a million dollars which he used to bribe IBM staff. After his arrest and trial, Hitachi had to pay IBM 60 times this sum in compensation.

# Counter-espionage

IN THE PAST, bugging equipment was often simple, and wires from hidden microphones sometimes led directly to eavesdropping spies. Today, finding bugs and wiretaps – and spies who use them – is harder. It is the job of counter-espionage, or counter-intelligence, agencies to track them down. However, detection of spies does not always lead to their capture – sometimes an enemy spy is more valuable if allowed to carry on as normal. Working spies can provide a counter-espionage agency with useful information, especially if they do not know they are being watched. A spy's activities can reveal an enemy's intelligence requirements and give away secrets about spying techniques and equipment. These details can be used to help trap other spies. Counter-intelligence services also use unmasked spies to feed false information to their enemies. Sometimes, by confronting spies with evidence of their guilt, a counter-espionage agency can "turn" the spies, forcing them to work against their original masters as double agents.

**SOMEONE IS WATCHING YOU**
Counter-espionage agencies use many of the same tools as the spies themselves. This 19th-century cartoon makes fun of the craze for hidden cameras among spies and counter-spies alike.

**KEEPING CALLS SECRET**
Devices called scramblers are sometimes used to keep telephone calls private. A typical scrambler breaks up speech into short segments, then rearranges these into an apparently random order for transmission down the telephone line. The "receiving" scrambler reverses the process. The people talking both use a scrambler, and they hear each other perfectly – but a spy who taps the line will hear nothing but "grey noise" (a meaningless jumble of sound).

Scrambler attached to telephone

**SETTING THE CODE**
A caller uses a row of tiny switches to set their scrambler to the same prearranged code as the receiving scrambler.

**COUNTER-SPY'S TOOLKIT**
When checking for bugs, the counter-spy uses screwdrivers and other basic tools to undo plug casings, and look behind light sockets and other likely places. A visual inspection can reveal damage left when a bug was installed. And by comparing every cable with a wiring diagram a counter-spy can confirm whether there are cables linking microphones to a distant transmitter.

*Rising tone in headphones indicates presence of a bug*

*Handle is removable to aid search of cramped spaces*

*Reducing power output helps pinpoint hidden bug*

*Probe detects bugs even when they are not transmitting*

**A NEW BROOM**
This device is used by a counter-espionage agent to quickly sweep (check) a room for bugs. The probe gives off a radio signal, which energizes semi-conductor devices, such as transistors or integrated circuits. This creates a tell-tale signal which the "broom" detects. Innocent electronic devices such as telephones will activate the detector, but once these are taken into account, any remaining signals probably come from a concealed bug.

255 — Strength of signal

0

20 MHz

Frequency

*Peaks indicate where there is a bug*

12 MHz

**LOOKING ROUND CORNERS**
Many offices have large spaces under the floor, above the ceiling and within the walls. These cavities are big enough to hide sophisticated and bulky monitoring equipment. To check such hiding-places, counter-surveillance staff use small mirrors and tiny lights. Flexible goose-necks on the handles allow the searcher to insert the mirror deep inside inaccessible places.

*Flexible goose-neck*

*Tiny mirror reaches in smallest holes*

**WHICH ROOM IS BUGGED?**
By displaying many scans from a tuned receiver in three-dimensional form, a room that contains a bug is revealed. The graph plots signal strength and frequency in megahertz (MHz) for each room of a building.

Cerberus 2
File Edit Radio View Windows Help
TEST            Location: 61      06/08/94 18:28
18.336M

*High peak indicates strong signal*

*This trace indicates the presence of a bug*

200

150

100

13.5M    16M    20M    23.5M
local oscillator frequency
signal strength

*Batteries in the handle power lamps*

*Portable computer visually interprets information from Scanlock receiver*

*Antenna picks up broadcast signals*

*Device makes high-pitched sound if it detects a bug*

**SCANLOCK DETECTOR**
Detecting cheap bugs is easy: play music in the suspect room, then use a radio receiver to scan commonly used frequencies until you hear the music. More sophisticated bugs avoid such counter-measures by broadcasting on unusual frequencies, by hopping between frequencies, or by scrambling their signals. This Scanlock wide-coverage tuned receiver picks up these "smart" bugs by scanning all the transmission frequencies within minutes.

**BUGS ON DISPLAY**
Connecting the Scanlock receiver to a portable computer displays its output in visual form. The jagged lines give a skilled operator much more information about radio signals in the surrounding area. Higher peaks indicate stronger signals. Each trace forms a picture of radio signal activity at one particular time. If a bug then switches on, its signal will change the shape of a later trace.

*Signal strength meter leads operator to bug*

**PINPOINTING A BUG**
Once counter-espionage agents are sure a room is bugged, they can use a lightweight signal-strength meter to track it down. These hand-held devices require no tuning and show a stronger signal the closer they are to the source.

# Spy-catching

LOCATING AND IDENTIFYING SPIES is rarely easy – unless a double agent or defector betrays them. Suspicious radio signals can sometimes allow counter-intelligence agents to pinpoint a hidden transmitter. By tapping telephones and secretly opening mail a counter-spy can find a few, and patient surveillance catches many more. Careless spies can give themselves, and others, away when collecting intelligence. For example, following a suspected spy sometimes leads to the discovery of other unknown agents. Once they are caught they must be "neutralized". This means exposing them so they cannot work secretly, expelling them to their home country, or prosecuting and imprisoning them. In some countries neutralization can have a more sinister meaning – a bogus trial and a death sentence.

**BLEEPS TRACE MISSILE SECRETS**
A tip-off by a defector alerted Britain's MI5 to spy Frank Bossard (born 1912). They caught him by fixing a transmitter to the files he "borrowed" from his Air Ministry office. The beacon's radio bleeps led MI5 officers to where the spy was copying the documents.

*Probe fits through slit at top of envelope and jaws grip the letter*

**SUSPICIOUS SPY-CATCHER**
As counter-espionage chief of the CIA, James Jesus Angleton (1917–87) hunted spies for two decades. He trusted nobody, and suspected every defector of being a KGB double agent. He found few moles, however, and his intense suspicion slowed the agency's work. By ordering illegal mail interceptions he damaged his reputation and was sacked in 1974.

*Winding handle rolls letter into tight coil*

*Applying invisible crayon sticks powder to a surface*

*The Rosenbergs are taken from court after being convicted*

*By pulling handle agent pulls out letter*

**FLAPS AND SEALS**
Counter-espionage agents use tools like this to open letters, read them and replace them without tearing the envelope. This skill, known as "flaps and seals", allows them to monitor letters addressed to a spy. Letters posted by the spy, however, are much more difficult to intercept.

**ROUGH JUSTICE**
Harsh punishment of spies has sometimes aroused strong emotions. Julius and Ethel Rosenberg were caught giving secrets to the Soviet Union. They were the first American peacetime spies to be sentenced to death and many people begged for mercy for them. But the two Communist spies were condemned and finally died in the electric chair in 1953.

## CAUGHT IN THE ACT

Video surveillance can catch a spy at work, but checking tapes from many cameras is very time-consuming. This may change with the development of digital cameras linked to computers. Once the software has "learned" what certain spies look like, it can pick them out in a crowd and start video tapes running to track the spy's movements.

*Surveillance cameras can be used to track a suspect's movements*

*SMERSH agent's identity card*

*Ultraviolet light shows up anti-bugging seals*

## "DEATH TO SPIES"

The Soviet counter-espionage organization Smert Shpionam (roughly translated as "death to spies") was responsible for military security, and for catching spies within the country's intelligence services. The agency soon acquired the nickname "SMERSH".

## CHECKING SEALS

After a bugging sweep counter-intelligence agents use seals to secure "clean" areas. An ultraviolet lamp is used to show up the anti-bugging stickers to check they are not broken.

## RED-HANDED

By dusting secret files with these special powders (left), counter-intelligence agents can catch a spy who handles the material. Powder sticking to the spy's hands glows under light from sources such as the ultraviolet lantern (above right).

*Screen relays signals from satellite to track small craft off the Florida coast that may be carrying drugs*

## NEW WORK

Spy-catching no longer grabs headlines as it did during the Cold War, and former counter-espionage officers now find they have other duties. The CIA, for example, has established a counter-narcotics centre to co-ordinate the activities of the American intelligence organizations in the fight against drug trafficking.

*Powder is invisible in normal light when sprinkled on files*

# Spying without spies

THE WORK OF REAL LIVE SPIES – or HUMINT (human intelligence) – is both costly and slow, and if a spy is discovered this could embarass politicians. Fortunately there are some alternatives. Technical intelligence-gathering uses remote sensors which can do the spy's work from a distance. COMINT (communications intelligence); SIGINT (signals); ELINT (electronic) and IMINT (imagery) all provide valuable knowledge. Perhaps the most important is IMINT, which is the gathering of pictures from cameras and radar in spy aircraft and satellites. These provide amazing views of objects on the ground – some can even distinguish between civilians and soldiers. Just as satellites improve a spy's distant vision, technical intelligence far below makes other senses keener. Sea-bed hydrophones track the sound of enemy submarines and, like sensitive fingertips, seismographs detect the vibrations caused by atomic tests.

**SPY PLANES WITHOUT PILOTS**
*Darkstar* is a drone, or uncrewed aerial vehicle (UAV), developed in the United States. UAVs can take detailed air photographs of heavily defended enemy territory without risking a pilot's life.

**SPY SATELLITE LAUNCH**
Older spy satellites used film because the pictures produced were sharper than video. The film fell to earth in a capsule for collection and processing. Such spy satellites are still secret. This Soviet launch carries a civilian version into orbit.

Russian KFA satellite on ground after re-entry

**THE EARTH FROM SPACE**
Multi-spectral images give intelligence agencies very detailed pictures of war zones and military bases, but they do not show the landscape in true colours. In this image of Sarajevo in former Yugoslavia, electronic processing has made buildings stand out in pink. With greater enlargement, pictures can record objects as small as a truck.

*Sensors behind coloured windows view targets in both visible light and infrared*

*Engines power the Blackbird forward three times faster than the speed of sound*

**EYES IN THE SKIES**
American Keyhole 12 spy satellites can "see" objects as small as a grapefruit from a distance of 400 km (250 miles). No nation releases pictures of its spy satellites. However, this Earth observation satellite, which is used for map-making, is built in the same way. Radar imaging allows spy satellites to look straight through cloud cover and infrared sensors can even pick out heat shadows left by a missile launch. Multi-spectral cameras in the satellite make it possible to distinguish between real trees and camouflage.

*Aircraft is very light in weight to increase range*

*Cockpit is not pressurized: pilot breathes pure oxygen from a helmet*

66882

## U-2 SPY PLANE
The CIA welcomed this high-flying spy plane as a triumph when it first flew in 1955 because they believed it was more accurate and dependable, and could collect information faster, than any agent on the ground. The U-2 cruised at 12,200 m (40,000 ft), but this proved not high enough when a Soviet missile shot down one in 1960. The pilot was captured (pp. 38–39).

*Explosion was equivalent to an earthquake with a magnitude of 6.2 on the Richter scale*

ground up

## TRACING THE BIG BANGS
Seismographs make vibrations in the earth's crust visible as a trace on paper. Geologists normally use them to monitor earthquakes, but the instruments can also register underground nuclear tests on the other side of the world. In September 1949, United States intelligence analysts got their first firm evidence that the Soviet Union had developed the atom bomb from a trace like this one.

*Trace shows activity at the Soviet Union's Kazakhstan test site in central Asia*

## TAKING A CLOSE LOOK
This is a unique photograph taken in 1984 of a Soviet aircraft carrier under construction in a Black Sea shipyard. The picture shows the ship's hull being built in two separate sections. Computer enhancement and colour have improved the quality of the picture.

*Black paint is needed to dissipate heat, because friction with the atmosphere warms the plane to 427°C (800°F)*

## BLACKBIRD WITH SHARP EYES
The *Blackbird* reconnaissance plane was built to replace the U-2. Though designed in 1959, the two-seater still flies higher and faster than any other aircraft. It can cross the Atlantic in less than two hours, and photograph a country the size of Mexico in 13 hours. Lockheed developed the U-2, the *Blackbird*, and *Darkstar* at a top-secret plant in Nevada known as the "Skunk Works". *Blackbird*s collected intelligence for more than 20 years during the Cold War, but were mothballed (taken out of service) to save money in 1990. Five years later, the US Air Force reconditioned several of the aircraft, and once more began training aircrew to fly surveillance missions.

# Spying today

SPIES THRIVED IN THE COLD WAR. While it lasted the United States and the Soviet Union feared each other's bombs and missiles, and needed intelligence agencies to help keep the peace. But when the Cold War ended in the late 1980s, many spies lost their jobs. Intelligence agencies had to adapt quickly. They looked for new uses for the spies' special skills and equipment and some formed alliances with scientists. Instead of tracking submarines, America's secret hydrophone network listened into the sound of whales. Spies found that their skills in counter-espionage were just as useful in counter-terrorism. Intelligence agents who had trailed Cold War traitors now followed Colombian drug barons. However, not all spies welcomed the role of international law enforcer. Some saw different career opportunities in the new, more peaceful world. In the chaos that followed the break-up of the Soviet Union, Russian farmers had planted 100,000 fields with opium poppies. All they needed were the people who had the right international connections to distribute the heroin that they made from the poppy heads. There was only one choice: they recruited some of Russia's newly redundant spies.

**SKY HIGH EYE**
Satellite data helps environmentalists monitor climate change and loss of habitat because of human activity or natural disaster. Spy satellites take the sharpest pictures, but until recently these have been kept secret. Now the CIA is making its images available to the general public. They will give researchers a clearer picture of how earth has changed over the last 40 years.

**DRUGS ON THE STREET**
Intelligence agencies can collect information about the production and the smuggling of narcotics. However, the war on drugs does not end when shipments reach their destination. Kits like these (left) help agents catch drug dealers. The sprays quickly identify drugs wherever they are, avoiding the cost and delay of laboratory analysis.

**EVERCHANGING ROLE**
However much the world changes, there will always be a role for secret agents. Russia may no longer threaten the United States, but war now endangers Eastern Europe, and CIA agents have learned to speak the local Serbo-Croat language. US Secret Service agents also have an important role to play guarding the president.

*US Secret Service man protects President Bush at an anti-drug summit*

**DRUGS SNOOPER**
The war against drugs increasingly relies on American satellites that were once used to police nuclear weapon treaties. High above Colombia, a "spy in the sky" can identify jungle landing strips, drug laboratories and storage areas. Using information gathered by satellite pictures, Colombian soldiers swoop on the bases with helicopters and ground troops. They seized 20 tonnes of cocaine in a single 1994 raid.

*Shoulder bag conceals a machine-gun*

*Fuel rod contains pellets of nuclear material*

**FUELLING FEAR**
Terrorists need 7 kg (15.5 lb) of plutonium from a nuclear power plant to build a bomb, and workers in Russia's crumbling nuclear industry are happy to sell it. Intelligence services across the world cooperate in tracing this stolen plutonium and uranium.

*Plutonium sealed inside is highly poisonous, but radiation it emits is not a danger to bomb-makers*

*Lighter fuel capsules to add to flammability*

*Power source (4 x 1.5 volt batteries)*

*Timer circuit board*

*Timer switch*

*Indicator light*

*Power on/off switch*

**IRA BOMB**
In 1993 MI5 (Britain's counter-espionage agency) joined the police in the hunt for the IRA (Irish Republican Army) bombers. In the past the IRA has used weapons such as this fire bomb in its campaign to unite Northern Ireland (a British province) with the Irish Republic. MI5 now uses its skills to track down other activists, including some animal rights campaigners who also use fire bombs.

*Compartment containing incendiary device*

*Fire bomb was defused before it could go off*

**SHINING PATH**
Behind bars, Abimael Guzman no longer leads the Shining Path guerilla movement that terrorized Peru for more than 20 years, killing 25,000 people. Police used spy tactics to catch him in 1992, first collecting intelligence, and then staking out his apartment with agents in disguise.

**ORGANIZED CRIME**
In the United States, the FBI tracks spies and fights organized crime gangs such as the Mafia and Chinese Triads. Counter-espionage organizations such as MI5 in Britain, have only recently joined the police in the fight.

*Gamblers gather at the headquarters of New York's Hung Mon Association, which has direct links with Triad gangs*

# Famous spies

THE MOST SUCCESSFUL SPIES do not become famous. As soon as their work is complete, they disappear into the shadows. Wartime spies are the exception to this. When the fighting ends, they tell their stories and sometimes earn high honours. As a reward for her spying, and for undergoing torture and imprisonment, Odette Sansom received one of Britain's most important medals, the George Cross. Not everybody believed that she deserved it. Yvonne Cormeau (pp. 32–33) complained that other SOE agents got a lesser award because "we haven't been caught". Of course all spies try to avoid capture, but if it happens fame can follow quickly. Their captors are eager to put the spies' crimes on show. Spy trials often disappoint newspaper readers who follow them – in a real spy's life glamour is rare, and the routine boring. However, a few spies do live lives as exciting as any novel. Some actually turn into fictional characters: Ian Fleming based James Bond on the spy Dusko Popov.

Sean Connery as Bond in the film of *Dr No*

**WILL THE REAL SPY STAND UP?**
Fictional James Bond (top) and real spy Dusko Popov (above with his wife) both enjoyed gambling and the company of beautiful women. Bond's creator, Ian Fleming (pp. 58–59) met Popov in 1941 when they were both secret agents.

*For her stage act, Mata Hari wore elaborate costumes and headdresses, but often danced naked as well*

*Mata Hari falsely claimed to be the daughter of a temple dancer and that she had been dedicated to the god Shiva*

**FAILED SPY**
As Mata Hari, exotic dancer Margaretha Macleod (1876–1917) entertained German officers in France during World War I. Although she became one of the most famous names in the history of espionage, she was not very good at spying. She was recruited by the German Secret Service, but they did not entirely trust her, and she offered her services to the Allies. Germany finally betrayed her to France and on 15 October 1917, she was executed by a French firing squad.

**CODENAME "WHITE RABBIT"**
Welsh Royal Air Force officer "Tommy" Yeo-Thomas became famous after his arrest and torture by the Gestapo, the German secret police, during World War II. He had been working for the SOE (pp. 32–33), organizing the French resistance to German troops occupying France. He was betrayed and captured outside a métro station in Paris. Tortured by the Gestapo, he was imprisoned but escaped from the death camp at Buchenwald in Germany.

*Forged papers gave "White Rabbit" cover stories on his visits to France*

Donald Maclean (1913–83) passed atom bomb secrets to Moscow

Guy Burgess (1911–63) attracted attention with his drunken violence

Kim Philby (1912–88) warned Maclean and Burgess when to flee

Anthony Blunt (1907–83) helped the others escape to the Soviet Union

*Odette Sansom was the first woman to win the George Cross*

Odette Samson with the dolls in 1954

*Dolls entirely hand-sewn*

*Ski sticks made from card and silver foil*

### WARTIME HEROINE
During World War II, Odette Sansom (1931–95) worked as "Céline", an agent for the Allied Special Operations Executive (SOE). She helped organize resistance groups in southern France. Betrayed by a double agent in 1943, Odette was captured and taken to Fresnes Prison near Paris where she was horribly tortured. After Fresnes, she was transferred to a prison in Germany and then to a concentration camp. Making these dolls for the nephew and niece of a German Catholic priest helped her pass the long hours of captivity. She was finally freed by the Allies in May 1945. The cruelty of her ordeal, and the valour with which she faced it have made her a legendary wartime spy.

### THE CAMBRIDGE FIVE
Four of this century's most notorious spies met at Cambridge University, England. While working for Britain's Foreign Office, Guy Burgess and Donald Maclean leaked secrets to Moscow, fleeing there in 1951 when MI5 began to suspect them. When the "third man" Kim Philby (pp. 34–35) joined them in 1961, a "fourth man", Anthony Blunt, secretly admitted to spying. In return for his confession, Blunt kept his job as Surveyor of the Queen's Pictures until he retired. However, by 1979, his name had become public knowledge and, later, a "fifth man", John Cairncross, was revealed.

### SHOW TRIAL VICTIM
Soviet military intelligence officer Oleg Penkowsky (1919–63) contacted Western intelligence agencies in 1960. He believed he could prevent war by telling the West about Soviet nuclear missiles. The secrets he provided gave the United States a real advantage in the Cold War. The KGB caught Penkowsky and he was given a show trial at which he "confessed". He was sentenced to death and reportedly executed in 1963.

# Spies in fiction

*Michael Caine played Harry Palmer in the 1965 film version of* The Ipcress File

Espionage has all the ingredients for an exciting storybook or movie: suspense, action, intrigue, and natural drama. American author James Fenimore Cooper (1789–1851) helped establish the spy story with his book *The Spy* in 1851, but spy novels have only really become popular in the last 50 years. Some of the most successful authors were themselves spies. Ian Fleming worked for British naval intelligence during World War II. John Le Carré drew on his experience of MI5 and MI6 to create a more authentic picture of the secret agent's world. Hollywood turned the books of both authors and many more into successful movies, but the books and films did not always impress real spies. Allen Dulles, once head of the CIA, wrote that "spy heroes ... rarely exist in real life". This did not stop the CIA from using spy films to train agents on the finer points and pitfalls of their trade.

### ANTI-HERO
In *The Ipcress File*, writer Len Deighton created a spy hero who shared only his nationality with James Bond. The story of the Cockney petty criminal turned reluctant spy was Deighton's hugely successful first book.

*Bond uses piton gun to fire rope during a spectacular bungee jump in the opening sequence*

*Grappling hook at end of rope*

### AUTHOR MEETS SPY
Frederick Forsyth (left) based his book *The Odessa File* on the exploits of the German "Champagne Spy" Wolfgang Lotz (right). Lotz crippled the Egyptian missile programme, helping Israel win the Six Day War against Egypt in 1967.

*Lotz's high lifestyle earned him his nickname of "the Champagne Spy".*

### SPY HIT LIST
British spies may not be the world's best, but the country's espionage writers top the best-seller lists. In the 1960s, their anti-Communist message alarmed the KGB. The Soviets hit back with *The Zakhov Mission*, in which a communist hero defeats 007. It could not compete with the success of Fleming's originals, which have been translated all over the world.

### FICTIONAL EVIL LADY
"We are enveloped in a network of spies," cries D'Artagnan, the young hero who helps the three musketeers in the famous adventure story written by Alexander Dumas (1802–1870). Milady (right) is the most deadly of the spies who are employed by Cardinal Richelieu (pp. 40–41) to try and discredit the Queen of France.

## INDIAN ROPE TRICK

High-tech gadgetry is as much the star in a Bond film as 007 himself. In the Bond books, Ian Fleming based these devices on genuine inventions supplied by people such as Charles Fraser-Smith to World War II agents (pp. 12–13).

*Buckle conceals 27-m (75-ft) long fine rope which can bear Bond's weight*

Bond's belt worn in the film *Goldeneye*

*Telescopic sights*

## TIME TOOL

Watches play a leading role in many of the Bond films. In *Goldeneye*, a laser built into Bond's watch helps him cut his way out of difficult situations. The KGB studied James Bond films in order to develop their own spy technology.

James Bond's piton gun from the film *Goldeneye*

*Piton gun contains laser which Bond uses to cut open the roof of a Russian chemical plant*

## LICENSED TO PRINT MONEY

When Ian Fleming (1908–64) created the character of James Bond, he was aiming to write the spy story "to end all spy stories". He succeeded. The 12 Bond books sold more than 18 million copies.

*In Goldeneye, the seventeenth James Bond film, Pierce Brosnan plays the sophisticated British spy*

*Bond primes a magnetic mine to destroy the chemical plant*

*The buggist's true-to-life tool kit includes lock-pick gun*

## BUGGED BATHROOM

In the film *The Conversation*, a bugging expert (played by Gene Hackman) is drawn into a terrifying world of deception and murder. As nerve-wracking as any political spy story, the film is a rare and authentic glimpse of the work of industrial espionage agents.

# Index

---

# Acknowledgements

**Dorling Kindersley would like to thank:**
Audiotel International Limited (Keith Penny, Ray Summers, Julie Walker, Adrian Hickey); Eon Productions (Julie O'Reilly); the Imperial War Museum, London (Paul Cornish, John Bullen, Mike Hibbard); Intelligence Corps Museum, Ashford (Major R.W.M.Shaw, Mrs. Janet Carpenter); Leica UK Ltd (Peter Mulder); Lorraine Electronics Surveillance (David Benn, Simon Rosser); Next Retail Ltd (Shirley Brown, Hilary Santell); Joanne Poynor; Spycatcher (Mike Phillips); Whitbread plc (Nicholas Redman, Archivist)
**Design help:** Ann Cannings, Jason Gonsalves, Sailesh Patel
**Pigeon:** Rick Osman
**Pigeon parachute:** Martine Cooper
**Artwork:** John Woodcock
**Endpapers:** Iain Morris
**Index:** Marion Dent
**Picture credits**
The publisher would like to thank the following for their kind permission to reproduce the photographs:
(a = above, b = below, c = centre, l = left, r = right, t = top)

**AKG Photos, London** / J.V. Leffdoel *Scipio Publius Cornelius* 40tl. **Ancient Art & Architecture Collection** 8tl, 8bl, 8bc. **Associated Press Ltd** 11tr, 29bl, 35t, 35br, 43c, 47bl, 52tr; Wire Photo 53cr. **Aviation Photographs International** 38tl. **Bildarchiv Preussischer Kulturbesitz** 25cl. **Bilderdienst Süddeutscher Verlag** 27cl. **Bridgeman Art Library** / Guildhall Art Gallery, Corporation of London, Sir John Gilbert, detail from *Ego Et Rex Meus* 40cl; Private Collection, I. Glasunov *Ivan The Terrible* 1989, 40bl; by courtesy of the board of Trustees of the V & A, London, Nicholas Hilliard, *Mary Queen of Scots* 28cl. **Camera Press Ltd.** 35tr, 39cl; R. Artacho 55br; S. Ferguson 42br; B Ross 56ra. **Jean-Loup Charmet** / Bibliothèque des Arts Decoratifs, Lucien Laforge *L'Espion*, 1916, 31tc. **D C Comics Inc.** *Spy vs Spy* is a trademark of E.C. Publications, Inc. ©1995. All rights reserved. Used with permission 42t. **Mary Evans Picture Library** front flap tl, 29r, 40c; J. Mammen back cover tl, 14tl. **E.T. Archive** / Biblioteca Nazionale Marciana, Venice 9tr; Musée Versailles, Philippe de Champaigne,

detail from *Cardinal Richelieu* 41cr; Staatliche Glyptothek, Munich 9tl; V & A, London 11tl. **Werner Forman Archive** / Ninja Museum Ueno, detail showing Ninja making secret signs 40bl; E. Strouhal 8bl. **Ronald Grant Archive**, *Stakeout* 1987, Touchstone 16bl, *Doctor No*, 1962, UA / Eon 56tr, *The Ipcress File* 1965, Rank / Steven Lowndes 58tr, *The Three Musketeers* 1948, MGM 58br, *The Conversation* 1974, Paramount / Francis Ford Coppola 59bl. **Keith Hamshere** front cover bcl, 4cb, 9br, 59tr, 59cr, 59br, 58-59. **Michael Holford** / Musée de Bayeux 8-9; V & A, London 10-11. **Hulton Deutsch Collection** 10cr, 38c, 41c, 41bl, 56l, 57tc, 57br, 57l. **Imperial War Museum, London** 23bc, 29tl, 36tr, 56br; Fougasse *Careless Talk Costs Lives* 10tr. **Lockheed** 52-53. **Lockheed Martin Skunk Works** 53t. **Magnum Photos Ltd** / E. Erwitt 43cl; S. Meiselas 54bl; E. Reed 19cr; A. Webb 51br; Zachmann 55bl. **The Mansell Collection** 10tl. **H. Keith Melton** front cover br and bcr, back cover rcb, 13tc, 28tl, 28cr, 28tr, 28br, 30br, 37tl, 37b, 42bl, 43br, 45tl, 51cl; Jerry Richards of the FBI Laboratory, Washington DC 10cl, 10c; Jack Ingram, Curator of the National Cryptologic Museum, Maryland 16cl, 16c, 27tr. **Mirror Syndication International** 27b, 50tr; Aldus Archive 24tl; Aldus Archive / Science

Museum / Eileen Tweedy front cover cr, 24cl; Rijksinstituut voor Oorlogsdocumentatie 9c; National Archives, USA 26c; Public Record Office 25tl, 41tl; © US Army 27tl. **National Cryptologic Museum, Maryland** 26bl. **National Portrait Gallery, London** / John De Critz, the Elder *Sir Francis Walsingham* 41tr. **Peter Newark's American Pictures** 30tl, 30bc, 31bl. **Popperfoto** 23tl, 31tr, 31br, 35bl, 41br, 58cl; Reuter / S. Jaffe 34br; Reuter / W. McNamee 34c. **Press Association** 36bcl. **Range** / Bettmann / UPI 22bl, 50c, 54br; Bettmann / UPI / Sam Schulman 50bc. **Rex Features Ltd** / Action Press 38-39; Sipa-Press 39tl. **Reuters Television** front cover tl, 42cr (detail), 54tl (detail). **Science Photo Library** / NRSC Ltd 52tl; R. Ressmeyer, Starlight 38bc. **Science & Society Picture Library, Science Museum, London** 26tl. **Frank Spooner Pictures** / Gamma-Liaison 11cl. **Topham-Picturepoint Ltd** back cover br, 12tl, 35cla, 35c, 34tl, 34tr; AP 45tc. **Worldmap-Priroda** 52tl, 52bl.

Every effort has been made to trace the copyright holders. Dorling Kindersley apologizes for any unintentional omissions and would be pleased, in such cases, to add an acknowledgement in future editions.